Lernkrimi English History

W0056002

DEATH OF A
DANDY

Barry Hamilton

Compact Verlag

Bisher sind in dieser Reihe erschienen:
- Compact Lernkrimi Englisch, Französisch, Italienisch, Spanisch:
  Grundwortschatz, Aufbauwortschatz, Grammatik, Konversation
- Compact Lernkrimi Englisch GB/US: Grammatik, Konversation
- Compact Lernkrimi Business English: Wortschatz, Konversation
- Compact Lernkrimi Deutsch: Grundwortschatz, Grammatik

In der Reihe Schüler-Lernkrimi sind erschienen:
- Compact Schüler-Lernkrimi Englisch, Französisch, Spanisch, Latein
- Compact Schüler-Lernkrimi Deutsch: Grammatik, Aufsatz
- Compact Schüler-Lernkrimi Mathematik, Physik

In der Reihe Lernthriller sind erschienen:
- Compact Lernthriller Englisch:
  Grundwortschatz, Aufbauwortschatz, Grammatik, Konversation

In der Reihe Lernstory Mystery sind erschienen:
- Compact Lernstory Mystery Englisch:
  Grundwortschatz, Aufbauwortschatz

In der Reihe Lernkrimi History sind erschienen:
- Compact Lernkrimi English History:
  Grundwortschatz, Aufbauwortschatz, Grammatik, Konversation

In der Reihe Hörbuch Lernkrimi sind erschienen:
- Compact Hörbuch Lernkrimi Englisch:
  Geübte Anfänger, Fortgeschrittene

Weitere Titel sind in Vorbereitung.

© 2007 Compact Verlag München
Alle Rechte vorbehalten. Nachdruck, auch auszugsweise,
nur mit ausdrücklicher Genehmigung des Verlages gestattet.
Chefredaktion: Dr. Angela Sendlinger
Redaktion: Gesa Füßle
Fachredaktion: Robert Laversuch
Produktion: Wolfram Friedrich
Titelillustration: Karl Knospe
Typographischer Entwurf: Maria Seidel
Umschlaggestaltung: Carsten Abelbeck

ISBN 978-3-8174-7660-2
7276602

Besuchen Sie uns im Internet: www.compactverlag.de

Vorwort

Mit dem neuen, spannenden Compact Lernkrimi History können Sie Ihre Englischkenntnisse auf schnelle und einfache Weise vertiefen, auffrischen und überprüfen.

Fesselnde Ereignisse im England vergangener Zeiten machen das Sprachtraining zu einem aufregenden und abwechslungsreichen Erlebnis.

Der Krimi wird auf jeder Seite durch vielfältige und kurzweilige Übungen ergänzt, die das Lernen unterhaltsam und spannend machen.

Prüfen Sie Ihr Englisch in Lückentexten, Zuordnungs- und Übersetzungsaufgaben, in Buchstabenspielen und Kreuzworträtseln!

Ob im Bus oder in der Bahn, im Wartezimmer, zu Hause oder in der Mittagspause – das Sprachtraining im handlichen Format bietet die ideale Trainingsmöglichkeit für zwischendurch.

Schreiben Sie die Lösungen einfach ins Buch!

Die richtigen Antworten sind in einem eigenen Lösungsteil zusammengefasst.

Und nun kann die Spannung beginnen ...

Viel Spaß und Erfolg!

Die Ereignisse und die handelnden Personen in diesem Buch sind frei erfunden. Etwaige Ähnlichkeiten mit tatsächlichen Ereignissen und historischen oder lebenden Personen wären rein zufällig und unbeabsichtigt.

Inhalt

Story

Philipp Havisham genießt im viktorianischen London ein abwechslungsreiches Leben. Er trifft seine Freunde im Klub, besucht Ruderrennen und lässt kaum eine Gelegenheit aus, schönen Damen den Hof zu machen. Sein unbeschwertes Dasein nimmt jedoch ein plötzliches Ende: Ausgerechnet in seinem Lieblingslokal wird er ermordet.

Detective Carlyle von Scotland Yard übernimmt die Ermittlungen. Bald deckt er auf, dass Havisham nicht nur Freunde hatte: Mit seinem Buch „Bekenntnisse eines Dandys" hat er die Frommen und Gottesfürchtigen der Gesellschaft gegen sich aufgebracht.
Als Detective Carlyle bei einem unheimlichen Pfarrer und seinem Gefolgsmann schier untrügliche Beweisstücke sicherstellt, scheint der Fall zunächst gelöst. Bis eine neue Spur auftaucht …

Chapter 1: A Dandy's Life

It was a mild morning as Philip Havisham stepped out of his house on Grosvenor Square, a large garden square in the exclusive Mayfair district of Victorian London. He picked up a newspaper from his doorstep. It was dated July 6, 1879. The headlines said "Zulu War Over!" Philip Havisham looked up. A coach drawn by horses approached his house, the horses' hooves drumming rhythmically on the cobbled street. The coach stopped in front of his gate. A well-dressed man in his late twenties stepped out. He tipped his top hat. The two men smiled at each other.

"I say, you're up early my dear friend!" beamed Philip Havisham.

"Well, you know what they say: 'The early bird catches the worm'," laughed Simon Manlove. They warmly shook hands.

"So, what brings you here so early, Simon?"

Mr Manlove looked surprised.

"Have you forgotten today's rowing competition on the Thames?"

"Oh yes, great, I forgot!" said Philip Havisham excitedly. "Come in, come in!"

The two friends entered the house.

"Wait in the drawing-room. I'll be back in a minute, help yourself to a drink."

Übung 1: Lesen Sie weiter und setzen Sie die Wörter in Klammern richtig ein!
(bright, room, glasses, stairs, pour, peace)

Philip Havisham disappeared up the (1.) _____. Simon Manlove entered the drawing-room. The wallpaper had an extravagant

ÜBUNG 1 !

pattern of birds and flowers. Its (2.) _____ colours of gold, red and green seemed to lighten up the (3.) _____. On a shiny round rosewood table was a tray with bottles of alcohol. Simon Manlove poured himself a gin. Shortly after, Philip Havisham entered the drawing-room.

"Would you kindly (4.) _____ me some of that exquisite port?"

His friend lifted up the port bottle and whistled.

"That must have cost you a pound or two!"

"Three to be precise," he answered ironically.

The companions lifted their (5.) _____.

"To my late wealthy father, may his soul rest in (6.) _____, if it were not for him I would not be able to live such a wonderful, breathtaking and immoral life."

"Yes, let us drink to your old man: one of the most successful Company Promoters of his time."

They laughed and clinked glasses.

"Cheers!"

Simon Manlove took his golden pocket watch out of his waist jacket pocket.

"Drink up then and let's go. The race starts in half an hour." Philip Havisham downed his port.

"Yes, let's go. This is going to be a lot of fun."

Übung 2: Lesen Sie weiter und unterstreichen Sie acht Begriffe, die mit Wasser zu tun haben!

Philip Havisham and Simon Manlove arrived just in time. Mr Havisham was in a very good mood. He rubbed his hands together joyfully.

"I never like to miss a rowing competition on the Thames."

"Yes, it's always such a great spectacle."

"And so full of life."

The men got out of the coach, which had stopped right beside the river. The water was full of boats and the riverbank was crowded. Crowds of spectators stood at the different landing stages along the Thames. Men, women and children cheerfully and eagerly awaited the beginning of the race.

"What a great atmosphere. I could do with a drink, what about you?" asked Simon Manlove.

"You know me, I never say no."

They swiftly walked towards a stand selling beer and tobacco. People turned around and looked at Philip Havisham. Some of them whispered or smirked, others just shook their heads. This was always the case as Philip Havisham liked to wear extravagant clothes. He never left the house without one of his long, shiny colourful scarves which he wore boldly around his long thin aristocratic neck. It fluttered in the mild summer breeze like an exotic flag. His top hat was elegantly tipped to one side and he never went anywhere without his shiny white cane made of pure ivory.

"Just arrived and you are already the centre of the show, Philip."

"Well, one does what one can."

Simon Manlove ordered two beers. The companions took their drinks and wandered along the riverbank. Groups of watermen had gathered at the different stairs which led into the river.

They were eagerly discussing the qualities of the individual boat race participants.

"Who do you think shall win?" Philip Havisham asked one of the men.

"I think the men rowing the boat called 'Sullivan' have a good chance, sir."

"A toast to Sullivan!"

Their glasses clinked. Mr Manlove and Mr Havisham moved on.

Übung 3: Finden Sie das passende Gegenteil und setzen Sie die richtige Ziffer ein!

1. crowded	☐ cold
2. good	☐ move
3. mild	☐ empty
4. bold	☐ lose
5. long	☐ cowardly
6. stop	☐ evil
7. win	☐ short

"Where are John and Stewart?"

"They should be here soon. I told them to meet us at this landing stage, and you have the best view from here."

"I hope they hurry up or they'll miss out on all the fun."

Just at that moment a man came hurrying towards them; he was very tall and slim. His long curly whiskers were perfectly groomed.

"Sorry I'm late, chaps. I had some important business to attend to."

Stewart Portman smiled and greeted his friends warmly.

"Where's John?" asked Philip Havisham.

"He didn't want to come to the race. You know he has been trying to avoid the Thames ever since Susan drowned herself in it."

"Poor soul, that really got to him," said Simon Manlove sympathetically.

"It was over a year ago, you would think he might have got over it by now," said Philip Havisham in a less sympathetic tone.

"Now that's not very fair, Philip…"

Suddenly there was a gun shot. The three men anxiously turned round and looked towards the distant bridge. As far as one could see, heads were bent forward and everybody had stopped talking and was looking in the same direction.

Übung 4: Übersetzen Sie und enträtseln Sie das Lösungswort!

ÜBUNG 4 !

1. Kutsche   _ _ ☐ _ _

2. viktorianisch   _ _ _ _ _ ☐ _ _ _

3. hell   _ _ ☐ _ _ _

4. Pferd   _ _ _ ☐ _

5. es   _ ☐

6. Haus   _ ☐ _ _ _

7. weil   _ _ ☐ _ _ _ _

8. Vater   _ _ _ _ _ ☐

9. Frieden   _ _ ☐ _ _

10. kosten   _ _ _ ☐

Lösung: _ _ _ _ _ _ _ _ _

"The boats are coming!" shouted Philip Havisham excitedly without taking his eyes off the bridge. The first boat shot under the bridge; followed by another and another.

"Here they come!" shouted Simon Manlove.

"Hooray!" cried the crowd around them.

The rowers came nearer. It was a close race. There was not a boat's length between the leading two. Philip Havisham took off his hat and turned it over.

"Okay, friends, the bets are on!" He threw in a pound note. "One pound on 'Sullivan'!"

Simon Manlove did the same and put his pound in the hat.

"One pound on the blue boat!"

Stewart Portman hesitated.

"What's wrong, Stewart?" asked Philip Havisham.

"You know betting is against the law."

"Oh, come on. It's just for fun. Don't be a spoil-sport!"

"If you insist." Stewart Portman looked in the direction of the boats and reluctantly placed a pound in Havisham's hat.

"I will bet on the red boat."

"Good on you, old boy."

ÜBUNG 5

! *Übung 5: Welche Wörter gehören zusammen?*
Setzen Sie die richtige Ziffer ein!

1. rowing	☐ driver
2. horse	☐ net
3. coach	☐ paddle
4. canoe	☐ skate
5. ice	☐ rider
6. fishing	☐ boat

Philip Havisham clapped his friend on the back. By this time the boats were nearly at their level. The shouting became very intense. People were hollering: "Come on Red, you can do it!" or "Sullivan for ever!" The boats darted by, Sullivan was leading; its rowers were using every muscle in their body to defend the lead they had gained. The men looked very strained. Minutes later the race was over. Sullivan had won. Philip Havisham happily took the three pounds out of his top hat. "Some you win, some you lose!"

He smiled at his friends. They smiled back.

"Don't worry, your money will be invested in a good cause. After I have bought us another round of drinks, I am going to take you all out for a meal. But first of all let us see if we can find some lady acquaintances."

Simon Manlove grinned knowingly. Stewart Portman smiled awkwardly.

"Don't worry my friend. They won't bite!" said Philip Havisham with a laugh and walked ahead. His companions shrugged and followed.

Übung 6: Welche Synonyme gehören zusammen?

1. win   ☐ succeed
2. smile   ☐ far
3. shout   ☐ grin
4. enter   ☐ near
5. distant   ☐ cry
6. good   ☐ go in
7. close   ☐ excellent

Philip Havisham and his friends eventually arrived at their favourite eating place called "Criterion" in the early evening. The three companions managed to persuade John Pirrip to come along. They had picked him up from the Royal Academy of Music, where he studied to play the

violin. The Criterion restaurant was located at Piccadilly Circus. Many aristocrats and well-to-do people came to eat there. Philip Havisham liked this expensive establishment very much. He liked everything that was costly and luxurious. He just loved to pass time smoking pricey cigars, drinking exquisite wines and eating first class food.

"Good evening, Gentlemen," said the director of the Criterion, Mr Green, as the young men walked through the entrance.

"The same table as usual?"

"Yes, please! I do like the East Room. It's so cosy and private," answered Philip Havisham.

A waiter came and took their coats.

He noticed John Pirrip's violin case.

"Shall I take your violin case to the cloak-room, too, sir?"

"No, thank you, we never part," answered John Pirrip.

"As you wish, sir," said the waiter and left.

The men passed the ante-room. Philip Havisham glanced in. The room had green and cream walls and large brass mirrors. Its comfortable dark leather chairs looked very inviting. He suddenly stopped. His eye had caught an extremely attractive woman in her early twenties. She also saw him and smiled.

"I will be with you in a minute," he said to his friend Stewart.

Stewart Portman saw the woman and put two and two together. He shook his head disapprovingly and said, "But don't take all night, Philip, we're rather hungry."

Übung 7: Beantworten Sie die Fragen zum Text!

1. What is the restaurant called?

ÜBUNG 7

2. Where does John Pirrip study?

_____

3. What instrument does he play?

_____

4. What kind of people dine at the Criterion?

_____

5. What does Philip Havisham like about the East Room?

_____

6. Where does the waiter take the men's coats to?

_____

7. Who does Philip Havisham see in the East Room?

_____

The group of friends moved on. Philip Havisham casually walked into the ante-room towards the young lady.

"Good evening, Patricia. You're looking beautiful as ever."

He kissed her hand.

"Good evening, Philip. And you are as charming as ever."

"What brings you to London? I haven't seen you in a long time." Patricia Gillian sighed and rolled her eyes.

"I know, I know. Ever since my Aunt Dorothy has taken over my marital affairs I don't get out a lot." Miss Gillian gave Philip Havisham a seducing look. "She is trying to protect me from men of your kind until Mr Right turns up and marries me."

"So where is the old bat? She doesn't seem to be doing such a great job."

A malicious smile flickered over her face.

"She is right behind you!"

Philip Havisham turned around. An elderly lady stood in front of him. She was very tall. A large diamond necklace covered her wrinkled décolleté. The woman looked at Philip Havisham sceptically.

"Mr Havisham, what a pleasure to meet you here."

The way she said this did not sound very convincing.

"How do you do?"

Her voice had a slight threatening touch to it.

"Very well, thank you, Lady Broughton. I cannot complain."

"So you have not wasted the fortune of your late hard-working father yet?"

Philip Havisham tried to keep smiling. He was just about to say something when Lady Broughton said, "Well, it was nice speaking to you. Have a nice evening."

And with this Lady Broughton took her niece's arm and pulled her discreetly away.

Philip Havisham cleared his throat.

"It was nice speaking to you, too, Madame."

Patricia Gillian turned around and waved. Philip Havisham waved back and then headed for the exit.

! *Übung 8: Welche Wörter gehören in die Lücken?*
(boatman, waiter, musician, husband, charm, royal)

1. A _____ serves in a restaurant.

2. A _____ plays an instrument.

3. A _____ is the male equivalent of wife.

4. A _____ rows a boat.

5. An aristocrat is of _____ descent.

6. A dandy has a lot of _____.

Philip Havisham walked along the long corridor leading to the East Room. As he entered he could hear the cheerful voices of his companions. This brought back a smile to his face.

"Some you win, some you lose!" he thought.

The East Room in the Criterion only had three tables and his favourite table was hidden by a wooden screen. The group of friends liked their privacy and met there every week to discuss art, literature, philosophy and other pleasures of life. Philip Havisham sat down beside his friends. They were already drinking a bottle of expensive French red wine. Simon Manlove filled up Philip Havisham's glass.

"Any luck?" he asked casually.

"No, I am afraid we were disturbed by her most ghastly aunt!"

"Lady Broughton?"

"Yes!"

"They say she used to be very beautiful in her time."

"Well, her time is most certainly over," Philip Havisham said bitterly.

"Look, we've already chosen tonight's menu," said John Pirrip changing the subject. He handed him the carte.

Philip Havisham's face brightened up. "Oh, lovely!"

Philip Havisham read the menu out loud.

"Caviar, asparagus and leek soup, sole filet, grilled chicken in mustard sauce... Mm, this is delicious!"

Mr Havisham lifted his glass.

"To friendship, the only thing that lasts."

"Hear, hear!" his friends replied.

! *Übung 9: Übersetzen Sie folgende Sätze!*

1. Das Restaurant hatte nur drei Tische.

_____

2. Er hörte ihre fröhlichen Stimmen.

_____

3. Sie tranken eine Flasche Wein.

_____

4. Man sagt, sie sei einmal sehr schön gewesen.

_____

5. Er las das Menü.

_____

6. Hast du Erfolg gehabt?

_____

7. Herr Havisham erhob sein Glas.

_____

The four gentlemen had a wonderful meal. They were just waiting for dessert when suddenly a tall young man appeared from behind the wooden screen and threw a book on the table. It landed with a loud bang straight in front of Philip Havisham and knocked over his full glass of wine. Astonished, the men looked at the rude intruder. His face was red with anger and his mouth twitched under his long, curled moustache.

"This novel is outrageous, absolute filth. You should be ashamed of yourself," the stranger shouted.

Philip Havisham calmly wiped his wet trousers with his napkin and said with an arrogant sneer, "May I know who my fierce critic is?"

"It's none of your business who I am!" answered the man.

"Well, you obviously don't seem to like my book, do you?"

"You can say that again, it's full of lies! If I didn't know better I would…"

The man tried to move on Mr Havisham, but his friends got up straight away and held him back. "Here's to you, Philip!" they shouted.

"Let me go you bunch of scum!" the man shouted.

At this moment Mr Green appeared.

"Please, gentlemen, this is no place for a quarrel!" he whispered.

"I was just leaving!" said the stranger and left hastily. He flew into the evening sky.

Philip Havisham looked at his friends.

"Another one of these ignorant people, who do not appreciate a good piece of fiction," he said.

They all laughed. Mr Green smiled, shook his head and left as if nothing had happened. Stewart Portman pulled his pocket-watch out of his waist jacket pocket. Then he threw it onto the floor.

"It's getting late; I think I'd better go now."

"Me too," said Mr Manlove.

Philip Havisham looked disappointed. He was really happy they were leaving.

"But what about dessert?"

"I'm full as it is. And Mary is expecting me."

"Oh well, that leaves us down to two. Doesn't it, John?"

John Pirrip downed his wine in one. Afterwards his glass was full.

"Guess it does, Philip! But we still have lovely Jane, here." He stroked his instrument case.

"Yes, I assume that will be the only woman you will be holding in your arms tonight," laughed Philip Havisham.

Simon Manlove and Stewart Portman laughed as well, but John Pirrip just stared at Philip Havisham grimly. Everybody felt a little uncomfortable.

"Sorry, John!" he said. "I should watch my silly mouth…I'm really sorry."

"It's okay," said John Pirrip sadly.

Simon Manlove and Stewart Portman gave John Pirrip a reassuring clap on the back and said goodbye. Over a year ago John Pirrip's fiancée had drowned herself in the Thames. Nobody understood why. Her death was a great tragedy and mystery. John said nothing. He seemed to be lost in thought. Philip Havisham felt a little awkward.

"I'll go to the men's room", he said, "I'll be back soon."

John Pirrip lit his pipe, nodded and sat back.

! *Übung 11: Ordnen Sie die Wörter zu sinnvollen Sätzen!*

ÜBUNG 11

1. with anger red his face was

_____

2. calmly he trousers wiped his

_____

3. his wine in one downed he

_____

4. place a quarrel no is this for

_____

5. man to move tried the him towards

_____

6. understood why nobody

_____

7. awkward he felt

_____

Philip Havisham took his time. He was in no hurry to get back to his friend. It wasn't that he really felt sorry. He just hated to have depressed people around him. In his view life was too short for depression. He strolled around the building and walked by the entrance to the anteroom. He looked to see if he could spot any other acquaintances. He saw nobody he knew. Philip Havisham wandered on to the empty Great Hall where the statue of Shakespeare looked meditatively down upon him. He stood in the middle of the room with his back to the door.

"Shakespeare, what a man," he thought.

Suddenly the door behind him closed. Philip startled and turned around.

"Are you following me…?"

He had no time to finish his sentence. The last thing Philip Havisham heard was a dull, deadly bang.

Übung 12: Welche Adjektive werden gesucht? Setzen Sie ein!
(grim, tragic, awkward, sad, silly, short, dull)

1. He was not happy, he actually looked very _____.

2. Her face looked fierce and _____.

3. That was very stupid and _____ of you.

4. How _____, I am very sorry.

5. The man's trousers were above his ankles, they were very _____.

6. It was an _____ situation.

7. The bang was _____.

Chapter 2: Tracing Lord Spencer

The London Police arrived at the murder scene shortly after Philip Havisham's body was found. Detective Hamish Carlyle pushed his way through a group of shocked guests blocking the corridor that lead to the Great Hall of the Criterion. The London Police Detective had a very impressive appearance. He was a small, stout man with thick red hair. His hair was so wild; he even had trouble finding a bowler hat to fit him. His red bushy eyebrows guarded over his clever and flaming blue eyes. This made him look fierce and a little rough, but Detective Carlyle was actually a very friendly and good-natured person. All the way up the corridor you could hear him saying: "Excuse me, madame!" or "Oh, thank you, sir!"

Übung 13: Fügen Sie die Übersetzung der deutschen Wörter ein!

One could tell by his (1. Akzent) _____ that Detective Carlyle was not originally from London, but (2. aus) _____ Edinburgh. He rolled the "R" in sir and strongly accentuated

the "A" in madame – a sign that he was a native Scot. He was followed by a number of constables. They were not quite as polite as their (3. Chef) _____.

"Get out of the way!" they snarled. "This is a crime-scene, not a tea party!"

Mr Green came running towards Detective Carlyle, he was very tense. The men introduced themselves to each other.

"It's a great (4. Tragödie) _____ …," he stammered nervously as he walked (5. neben) _____ the detective. "I just don't understand…"

They entered the Great Hall. Philip Havisham lay on the (6. Boden) _____. His arms were spread out and his eyes wide (7. offen) _____. Blood trickled out of the area where his (8. Herz) _____ used to beat. Detective Carlyle took in the scene thoughtfully.

"Is there anything I can do?" asked Mr Green.

"Yes, close the restaurant for today, but don't let anybody leave before we question them," answered Detective Carlyle.

"But Detective Carlyle, very important people dine here; I just can't force them to stay."

"I know you can't force them, but I can. However, I'm sure your way is more diplomatic."

"What a day!" mumbled Mr Green nervously to himself and left.

Detective Carlyle stepped into the room and walked around the body. Sergeant Thompson arrived. He was Detective Carlyle's best

man and his features showed signs of great intelligence. Detective Carlyle liked him very much and was certain that one day he would become Chief Inspector.

ÜBUNG 14

Übung 14: Welches Wort ist das „schwarze Schaf"?
Unterstreichen Sie das nicht in die Reihe passende Wort!

1. snarl, bite, bark, smile
2. important, beggar, well-to-do, aristocratic
3. run, walk, stand, move
4. leave, go in, arrive, enter
5. great, terrible, good, super
6. pleased, happy, sad, cheerful
7. speak, talk, chat, silence
8. diplomatic, tactful, careless, careful
9. shocked, upset, happy, troubled
10. secure, vulnerable, safe, protected

"So what do you think?" Sergeant Thompson asked his superior.
"Certainly it looks as if the murderer is good with a gun. One shot straight in the heart. He probably died instantly."
"How is it that nobody heard the shot?" asked Sergeant Thompson.
Detective Carlyle walked to the corner of the room and pointed at a cushion with a hole in it.
"That's why; the murderer used a cushion to silence the gun."
"That old trick never fails, eh?" said the sergeant. "Is the cushion from this room?"
"I don't think so. I can't see any others."
Detective Carlyle looked up at the statue of Shakespeare.
"If only you could speak," he said quietly to himself.

At that moment Mr Green entered the Great Hall again. He was dabbing his sweaty bald head with a handkerchief.

"I did what you told me, but I must say, many of my guests are not pleased at all…"

Detective Carlyle ignored the last sentence. "Who found Mr Havisham's body?"

"His friend, Mr Pirrip. He's sitting in the ante-room. He appears to be in a state of shock. They had just dined together shortly before this…eh…incident."

Detective Carlyle looked at his sergeant.

"You secure the crime-scene, meanwhile I'll see to Mr Pirrip."

Übung 15: Übersetzen Sie!

1. zu Abend essen   _____

2. zu Mittag essen   _____

3. frühstücken   _____

4. Abendessen   _____

5. Mittagessen   _____

6. Frühstück   _____

The ante-room was crowded. There were smaller and larger groups of people standing around talking. The main topic was the death of Philip Havisham. A pale, thin man sat on a chair staring into the blazing fire. He was drinking a brandy. It was in fact his fifth or sixth. Detective Carlyle sat on the chair opposite him.

"Are you Mr Pirrip?"

"Yes!" he said without lifting his eyes from the fire.

"I thought so. May I introduce myself? I am Detective Carlyle from the London Police."

John Pirrip looked up. Both men shook hands.

"I heard Mr Havisham was a good friend of yours."

"Yes, that is true."

The young man seemed very miserable and sad.

"I know this is not quite the time, but I have a few questions I must ask you."

John Pirrip took a sip of his brandy and turned his face back to the fire.

"Go ahead."

Detective Carlyle took out his notebook and pen.

"Is it true that you found Mr Havisham in the Great Hall?"

"Yes!"

"How did this come about?"

John Pirrip took a deep breath.

"Well, he said he was going to the men's room. After about 25 minutes I started to wonder where he was. So I looked for him and as you know I eventually found him…", John Pirrip gulped, "…dead!"

Mr Pirrip downed his brandy.

*Übung 16: Vervollständigen Sie die Sätze mit **after** oder **before**!*

1. _____ about 25 minutes John Pirrip went to look for his friend.

2. _____ he went he poured himself another drink.

3. _____ John Pirrip found Philip Havisham he called the police.

4. Some time passed _____ he started to get worried.

5. _____ he could say another word he was dead.

6. The police arrived soon _____ he had called.

"Since you were close, do you have any idea who could have done such a thing?"

John Pirrip smiled bitterly.

"Philip had a lot of enemies. He wasn't what you would call a respected member of society."

"What do you mean?"

John Pirrip looked surprised.

"Haven't you heard of his book 'Dangerous Confessions of a Dandy'? It caused quite a scandal."

"No, what is it about?"

"It's a fictional story about the life of a dandy in London called Robert Sway and his experiences; it certainly does not shed a good light on Victorian society."

Detective Carlyle raised one of his bushy eyebrows.

"Does it not?"

"No, the novel unmasks society's bigotry and indirectly criticizes the church and the government. His debut has not made him very popular."

Übung 17: Ordnen Sie die Wörter ihrem Gegenteil zu!

1. popular	☐ happy
2. important	☐ true
3. fictional	☐ sweet
4. dangerous	☐ unpopular
5. bitter	☐ unimportant
6. miserable	☐ safe

"What makes you think the book has something to do with the murder?"

"Philip has received a few death threats recently…oh, and just half an hour before he was murdered this chap tried to threaten him because of the book. You should have seen him, he was very angry."

"Really?" the eyebrow went up again.

"Do you know who he was?"

"No, never seen him before. He just turned up out of nowhere, but maybe Mr Green knows him."

"Okay, thank you Mr Pirrip, that will do for just now."

John Pirrip nodded and stared back into the fire. Detective Carlyle got up, closed his notebook and said goodbye.

ÜBUNG 18

Übung 18: Welche der folgenden Aussagen sind wahr?
Markieren Sie mit richtig ✓ oder falsch – !

1. Philip Havisham and John Pirrip were good friends. ☐
2. Mr Green found Philip Havisham. ☐
3. Philip Havisham did not have many enemies. ☐
4. Detective Carlyle does not know Philip Havisham's novel. ☐
5. John Pirrip is drinking champagne. ☐
6. Philip Havisham was shot in the East Room. ☐
7. "Dangerous Confessions of a Dandy" is a true story. ☐

The detective fought his way back to the Great Hall. His constables were interviewing the guests one after another. They were listening, nodding and writing down anything that seemed important. "Come to any conclusions?" asked Detective Carlyle as he walked into the room. "Not really, sir," answered the sergeant. "And I can't find a gun, however I assume the victim was taken by surprise."

"Yes, the murderer may have followed him and waited for the right moment…or someone lured him to the Great Hall. What have your men found out, Sergeant, did anybody see anything suspicious?"

"No, but they have not yet questioned all of the guests."

Detective Carlyle bent over Philip Havisham's body.

"His wound is quite big. The gun certainly was not small. Maybe it was a Remington Revolver or a Colt. You certainly can't just walk into a restaurant with one of those in your pocket. Somebody must have seen something suspicious."

"We'll see what the autopsy says, sir. Dr Brown should be arriving any minute. He was playing a game of whist at Colonel Walkers, but one of my men eventually found him."

"I hope the man is sober. He is notorious for having a few drinks."

Mr Green entered the room. He was followed by a middle-aged, handsome looking man, who held a small black leather bag in his hand. It was Dr Brown. He seemed a little unsteady on his feet.

Übung 19: Verneinen Sie folgende Sätze!

1. Dr Brown was sober.

_____

2. He lost his balance.

_____

3. Detective Carlyle knows who the murderer is.

_____

4. The constables were listening.

_____

5. The sergeant's men have found a clue.

_____

"Good evening, Gentlemen. What do we have here?"

Dr Brown approached the body. He hiccoughed.

"Oh dear, if that is not the notorious dandy Philip Havisham," he said dryly.

"You know this man?" asked Detective Carlyle.

"Yes, from the newspapers. I read his book. I don't know what all the fuss is about, it's great."

Dr Brown smiled and kneeled down beside the body. He nearly stumbled, but managed to keep his balance.

"Have you been drinking, Dr Brown?" asked Detective Carlyle.

"Oh, just the usual night-cap."

"I bet!" whispered Sergeant Thompson to himself.

"I would like to know what kind of bullet killed him."

"No problem. I'll have him taken to the hospital as soon as you're finished here and pull it out. Good shot, eh?" chuckled Dr Brown.

The others did not think this very funny.

"Show some respect, Doctor!" said Sergeant Thompson.

Dr Brown seemed embarrassed.

"Ehm…well…yes…I guess you're right."

Dr Brown started to take medical instruments out of his bag.

Detective Carlyle shook his head and turned around to Mr Green. He was still very nervous.

"John Pirrip told me that someone had threatened Mr Havisham shortly before he was killed. Do you know the man?"

"Yes, his name is Lord Manuel Spencer."

Detective Carlyle wrote this information in his notebook.

"I think we'll visit Lord Spencer tomorrow, Sergeant Thompson."

"Very good idea, sir."

Übung 20: Benutzen Sie die Kurzform!

1. I cannot _____	6. it is _____
2. I will _____	7. could not _____
3. I do not _____	8. I am _____
4. you are _____	9. he is _____
5. we will _____	10. does not _____

Mr Green wanted to leave the Great Hall again.

"Oh, I have one last question, Mr Green."

Mr Green turned around.

"Yes!"

"Is this cushion part of the restaurants interior?"

Mr Green screwed up his face.

"I should certainly think not! It looks very shabby to me."

"Thank you, Mr Green. That will be all for now."

"For now?" said Mr Green uneasily. "I must say, I don't like the sound of that at all. This whole affair is a never ending story!"

Sergeant Thompson and Detective Carlyle looked at each other and shrugged.

"This is just the beginning," said Detective Carlyle knowingly.

Mr Green did not hear this because he had already gone.

Übung 21: Lesen Sie weiter und übersetzen Sie die Wörter in Klammern!

The next day Detective Carlyle and Sergeant Thompson went to

Lord Manuel Spencer's lodgings. They stood (1. vor) _____

a shabby second class London hotel called "Stephan's" on Hill Street just off Berkley Square.

"Are you sure this is the right place, Sergeant? It doesn't look like the home of an aristocrat to me."

"I see your point, but I'm certain he lives here."

The policemen (2. betraten) _____ the hotel. A man was sitting at the reception desk smoking a pipe and reading the newspaper. He looked up, startled as soon as he saw the policemen coming towards him.

"Good afternoon, can I help you?" he said apprehensively.

"We (3. hoffen) _____ so," answered Detective Carlyle.

"Is there a Lord Spencer staying here?"

"Lord Spencer?" said the landlord (4. überrascht) _____

"Do you mean Mr Manuel Spencer?"

"Yes!"

"Well he is staying here, but I haven't seen him since yesterday morning."

"He did not come home (5. letzte Nacht) _____?" asked Detective Carlyle with great interest.

"No!"

"You seemed surprised that Mr Spencer is of aristocratic descent?"

"Well, yes. He sometimes has (6. Geldprobleme) _____

and can't always pay his rent. Mr Spencer…I mean Lord Spencer certainly is not a wealthy man."

Sergeant Thompson looked around. Suddenly his (7. Auge) _____ caught something. He walked over to a chair placed in the reception area and lifted up a cushion.

"Look sir, it's the same cushion we found at the crime scene!"

"Well done, Sergeant Thomson!"

"Crime scene?! What crime scene?" asked the landlord nervously.

"We can't talk about it right now, however I am (8. neugierig) _____. Are you missing any of these cushions?"

"Ehm…no…I mean…I don't count them," stammered the landlord.

"Well maybe you could find out if any cushions of that kind are missing. In the meantime, I and my colleague would like to inspect Lord Spencer's room, please."

Detective Carlyle held out his hand. The landlord grabbed a key and placed it in the detective's hand.

"Room number 17. It's on the second floor."

"Thank you!"

The policemen unlocked the hotel room door and entered. The room was small and dusty. However, the room was very tidy. In one corner there was a single bed and in the other corner by the window there was a desk and chair. A typewriter was placed on top of the desk.

"Not the place you would expect to find a Lord, is it?" said Sergeant Thompson.

"No, it certainly isn't."

Detective Carlyle walked over to the desk and opened the drawers. He did not find anything suspicious. He bent down. Under the desk was a waste-paper basket full of paper scraps. Detective Carlyle emptied it on the floor.

! *Übung 22: Unterstreichen und verbessern Sie im folgenden Textabschnitt die acht falsch geschriebenen Wörter!*

ÜBUNG 22

"Let's sea what we have here."

Sergeant Thompson joined his superior. They started sorting out the paper scrapps.

"This is interesting!" said Detective Carlyle and read the content of a letter out loud, which he had just taken out of an envelope.

"Havisham is going to be at the Criterion this evning."

That is what the entire message said.

"Looks like somebody tipped off Lord Spencer. He new Havisham was going to be at the Criterion."

"That could mean that if Spencer has something to do with the murder he isn't in it alone."

Sergeant Thompson unfolded another peace of paper.

"Luke at this, sir! It's about some campain against Havisham's book."

He shoed it to Detective Carlyle.

1. _____   5. _____

2. _____   6. _____

3. _____   7. _____

4. _____   8. _____

It read: "Set an example for moral values now! Come to the book burning on July the 25th of 'Dangerous Confessions of a Dandy' written by Philip Havisham. Meeting place, church of St Andrews."

"I know that church. It's a very conservative Evangelical church near Fleet Street," said Sergeant Thompson.

"It's been typed on a typewriter. I wonder if Lord Spencer typed this himself."

Detective Carlyle saw that the letter "W" on the sheet of paper had a very specific malfunction.

"Put in a piece of paper in the typewriter and see if it types the 'W' in the same way."

Sergeant Thompson put a sheet of paper in the typewriter and pressed "W".

"You were right. He wrote the campaign letter on this typewriter. He sure hated Havisham's book and probably hated him also as much."

"I'm sure he did, but the question is: Did he hate him so much to want him dead?"

"Good question, sir. But you know what these religious fanatics can be like."

Übung 23: Fügen Sie die richtige Präposition ein!
(in, near, over, at, under, on)

1. The book was _____ top of the desk.

2. He walked _____ to him.

3. Scraps of paper were _____ the waste-paper basket.

4. The waste-paper basket was _____ the desk.

5. He was sitting _____ the reception.

6. The restaurant was _____ the police station.

The policemen went back downstairs. The landlord was expecting them anxiously.

"You were right. One of my cushions is missing."

He showed the policemen a chair in the hall near the doorway.

"That's very suspicious."

"It certainly is, Sergeant Thompson."

Detective Carlyle turned to the landlord and showed him the message he found in Lord Spencer's room.

"Did anyone give you this message for Lord Spencer?"

The man shook his head.

"No!"

"So Lord Spencer didn't receive any messages yesterday?"

"To be honest, he has never received a message."

"Very strange, very strange indeed. Did Lord Spencer have any visitors recently?"

"No, he never had visitors, either. That is…wait a minute! He did have a visitor once, about two weeks ago. The man was a cleric – a minister to be precise."

"Can you remember his name?"

"Sorry, I can't."

"What did he look like?"

"Scary!"

"Scary, what do you mean by that?"

"It's difficult to say, Detective. He was creepy. His face was as white as a sheet; he had very dark thick hair and was at least six foot ten. The man never smiled once."

Detective Carlyle's eyebrow went up.

"Really? Well, thank you for your help. Goodbye!"

"Goodbye!"

Back out on the street the two policemen discussed their next steps.

"Maybe the minister who visited Lord Spencer is the same minister from St. Andrews Church. It can't be a coincidence that the campaigners wanted to meet there," said Sergeant Thompson.

"Could well be. Maybe they organized the campaign against Havisham's book together."

The policemen decided to go to St Andrews Church.

Übung 24: Bilden Sie positive Sätze!

1. Lord Spencer didn't receive a message.

_____

2. He never had visitors.

_____

3. I can't.

_____

4. No, certainly not.

_____

5. No, thank you.

_____

6. I won't come.

_____

7. I don't care.

_____

Chapter 3: The Mysterious Minister Black

By the time Detective Carlyle and Sergeant Thompson arrived at St Andrews Church it was getting dark. The church was very old. On one side there was an ancient graveyard. The grave stones were worn and many of them sloped to the side. It was overgrown with grass and weeds.

"It's a creepy place and look at the graveyard; it looks almost like tombstones in a jungle."

The sergeant looked up at the roof of the church. Winged stone demons looked fiercely down upon them. He shivered.

"My father used to say: 'Scary places keep away unwanted guests'," said Detective Carlyle. "Let's have a look around."

The policemen opened the gate of the church yard. It squeaked loudly. Sergeant Thompson jumped with fright. Detective Carlyle smiled at him.

"I think it needs a little bit of oil."

"Yes, absolutely!" said the sergeant trying to play down his fear.

They found the entrance to the church. It was locked. The men moved on. Eventually they came to the minister's house. It looked just as creepy as the rest of the place.

"Somebody is at home, sir. There are some lights on in the first floor."

On the door it said: Minister Black. The policemen knocked at the door. They waited for a minute, but nobody answered.

UBUNG 25

Übung 25: Welche Wörter passen inhaltlich zusammen?

1. winged	☐ cleric
2. grave	☐ overgrown
3. church	☐ locked

4. house	☐ yard
5. door	☐ stone
6. garden	☐ demon
7. minister	☐ home

"Knock again, Sergeant, please."

There was still no reaction. The men looked up at the first floor.

Sergeant Thompson knocked at the door again, this time longer and harder. Eventually the door opened.

A very tall, pale man with thick black hair stood in front of them. He was dressed in ministers' clothes. The detective and the sergeant exchanged acknowledging looks.

"What do you want?" asked the minister in an unfriendly tone.

"Good evening, Minister," said Detective Carlyle nicely. "My name is Detective Carlyle from the London Police and this is my colleague Sergeant Thompson. We would like to ask you a few questions."

"Question's about what? I don't think I can help you!"

"That's up to us to decide. We are looking for a man called Lord Manuel Spencer. Do you know him?"

"Never heard of him!" he replied harshly.

"But we have a witness who claims you visited him at Stephan's Hotel."

"Stephan's Hotel? Never heard of the place and now if you would excuse me, I am a busy man."

The minister tried to close the door, but the sergeant put his foot in the way.

"Get your foot out of my door! You have no right to question me!" he said angrily.

"As I said, we have a witness," said Detective Carlyle calmly.

"A witness? Ha, whose word do you believe more: that of a landlord of some second class hotel or a man of God?"

The bushy red eyebrow went up again.

! *Übung 26: Bilden Sie die Pluralformen!*

ÜBUNG 26

1. witness	_____	6. half	_____
2. door	_____	7. sheep	_____
3. dress	_____	8. scarf	_____
4. lady	_____	9. day	_____
5. wife	_____	10. tooth	_____

"I don't believe anybody *more,* Minister. I just believe the truth. How do you know that Stephan's is a second class hotel?"

For a short second the minister looked irritated.

"It was a good guess, nothing more. Now if you would excuse me!"

The minister slammed the door in the policemen's faces. Sergeant Thompson whistled.

"What a bad tempered person."

"Yes, and what a bad liar, too. He definitely knows more than he is letting on. We'll have to come back another time."

The policemen made their way back to the gate. Just as they were passing the church they heard a loud crashing noise. Sergeant Thompson was startled.

"What was that?"

"I don't know. It came from inside the church."

The policemen went to the entrance.

"Open the door, please, Sergeant."

Übung 27: Setzen Sie **to** *oder* **too** *ein!*

1. He is not only a thief, he is a bad liar _____.

2. Minister Black lied _____ the policemen.

3. The minister ought _____ tell the truth.

4. Detective Carlyle has far _____ much work to do.

5. Lord Spencer used to be rich _____.

6. The case is getting _____ complicated.

The sergeant took out a long metal instrument with a hook at the end. He put it in the lock then twisted and turned it. There was a loud clacking noise and the church door opened. It was very dark inside, a lamp hung beside the door on the wall. Sergeant Thompson took it down and pulled a box of matches out of his pocket.

"This should brighten things up a little," smiled Sergeant Thompson and lit the lamp.

Detective Carlyle and Sergeant Thompson went in carefully. In a far corner the men could see piles of boxes. One of them had fallen against the altar.

"Do you think someone is in here?" whispered the sergeant.

"Maybe, keep your eyes open. First of all let's see what's in the boxes."

The policemen moved slowly towards the boxes; the sergeant keeping a watchful eye on everything around them. Detective Carlyle opened a box.

"Look, it's full of Philip Havisham's novel 'Dangerous Confessions of a Dandy'."

The detective opened another box and another. Sergeant Thompson followed him all the time with the lamp.

"Looks like Minister Black ordered a great amount of Philip Havisham's book and I doubt he did this because he is a great admirer," Detective Carlyle remarked.

"Probably for the book burning, sir," said Sergeant Thompson.

"Yes, I wonder how Minister Black is going to talk himself out of this one," said Detective Carlyle triumphantly.

! *Übung 28: Wählen Sie die richtige Alternative!*

1. The minister _____ opened the door.

   a) ☐ scarcely   b) ☐ immediately   c) ☐ eventually

2. He was a _____ - tempered person.

   a) ☐ well   b) ☐ bad   c) ☐ good

3. There were _____ of boxes.

   a) ☐ miles   b) ☐ masses   c) ☐ piles

4. Sergeant Thompson _____ a box of matches out of his pocket.

   a) ☐ pulled   b) ☐ placed   c) ☐ put

5. Keep your eyes _____.

   a) ☐ wide   b) ☐ large   c) ☐ open

6. Sergeant Thompson _____ Detective Carlyle.

   a) ☐ shadowed   b) ☐ trailed   c) ☐ followed

Suddenly the policemen heard another noise.

They turned around in the direction of the noise. Sergeant Thompson held up the lamp trying to cast more light.

"Is there anybody there?" he shouted. "This is the London Police. Come out and show yourself now!"

The sergeant's voice echoed and bounced off of the cold stone walls. There was no answer. The policemen held their breaths and listened.

"Maybe it was just a mouse or something, sir?"

"You could be right, but let's take a look."

The men moved slowly over to the corner where the noise had come from. Sergeant Thompson pulled out his truncheon.

"Nobody here!" The sergeant moved the lamp up and down, lightening up the walls and the floor.

"Wait a minute, Sergeant!" said Detective Carlyle all of a sudden. "Shine the light back onto the wall…no, not there, a little more to the left…yes, that's it."

"What is it, sir?" asked the sergeant astonished.

Detective Carlyle walked over to a stone in the wall that stuck out more than the others and pushed it. It gave way and part of the stone wall swung open.

"A secret passage!" said Sergeant Thompson bewildered. "But how did you know?"

Detective Carlyle smiled at him knowingly.

"I have come across the odd secret passage in my time and some things just never change."

The door opened up to a winding spiral wooden staircase.

"After you, Sergeant!"

Übung 29: Enträtseln Sie die folgenden Definitionen!

1. a place you pay to stay in: _____ (telho)

2. an aristocratic title: _____ (uked)

3. a large church: _____ (thcaraled)

4. a thing you can write letters with: _____ (pyteertwri)

5. something that happens by chance: _____ (ecnedicnioc)

6. a police rank: _____ (gresaetn)

7. an undisclosed corridor: _____ _____ (cesssterpaega)

8. something which creates light: _____ (malp)

9. an element of time: _____ (eminut)

10. the opposite of before: _____ (ertfa)

The men slowly walked down the staircase. The wooden stairs creaked under their feet. At the bottom of the steps the sergeant suddenly cried out loud: "Arrrggghhh!"

Detective Carlyle jumped with fright. He nearly fell down the stairs, but caught the railing in time.

"Are you alright, Sergeant?"

Detective Carlyle's voice was shaky, but he tried to keep calm.

"Sorry, sir, I'm alright. I didn't want to frighten you, but look at this…"

Sergeant Thompson shone his lamp along a long, thin corridor.

"Skeletons!" gasped Detective Carlyle.

As far as their eyes could see skeletons lay on stone platforms alongside both walls.

"This must be some kind of crypt," said Detective Carlyle.

The two men walked on, passing by the motionless bones that once had belonged to living human beings. Sergeant Thompson shivered. "These lads could do with a bit of sunlight, might ease the old bones a little," he joked, trying to laugh away his fear.

At the end of the corridor the policemen reached a door. Detective Carlyle opened it carefully. The men entered a small, square-shaped

chamber. It consisted of a desk and several shelves full of books. On the floor lay a mattress. A plate with fruit and food lay beside it.

"Looks as if someone has been sleeping here."

"Yes, probably somebody who does not want to be found." remarked Detective Carlyle thoughtfully and looked over to the desk.

"Shine the lamp over to the desk please, Sergeant."

The desk was untidy. Everything was neat. Sheets of paper were spread all over it. A fountain pen lay on top of the desk. Detective Carlyle lifted up one of the sheets and read it.

"What does it say?"

"It's a death threat and it's addressed to Philip Havisham." Detective Carlyle's red bushy eyebrow went up. He took a sip of tea. "I think we have a lead here, Sergeant – I definitely do! The books, the death threats; I think the minister has a lot to explain!"

"Do you think he has something to do with the murder?"

"I'm not quite sure yet, but something is certainly very fishy about the man. The boxes of books definitely prove that he knows Lord Spencer. They probably organized the book burning session together. If you ask me somebody has been hiding out here and I bet it was Lord Spencer."

Detective Carlyle looked up and saw a bell hanging from the roof.

"Look Sergeant, a warning system. The minister most likely informed Lord Spencer of our presence."

"I think Minister Black certainly has a few things to explain," said Sergeant Thompson.

With that the policeman headed back to the staircase. Just as they got to the top of the stairs they could here somebody running up the church isle. Detective Carlyle closed the secret passage.

"There's somebody in the church after all. I'll get him, sir!"

The sergeant run up the rest of the steps and shot out into the church. Detective Carlyle followed him in time to see a shadow dart out of the church door. It suddenly bent down and plucked a flower.

"Stop, in the name of the law!" shouted Sergeant Thompson as he ran in the direction of the exit. The bright sun almost blinded him.

The sergeant managed to catch up with the person fast. He was about 15 feet behind him. Sergeant Thompson jumped over a grave stone. The pursued man shot around to the right and headed for the church gate. Sergeant Thompson was very close now; he jumped and caught the fleeing man by the collar. They both fell to the ground. Sergeant Thompson got on top of the struggling man and held him down.

"Let me go, let me go!" he cried.

Shortly after Detective Carlyle arrived, he was puffing and panting.

"Good evening, Lord Spencer," he panted.

"You have no right…," he tried to throw the sergeant off of him. "Get this rogue off of me…"

"Now, now, now, Lord Spencer; you don't want us to charge you for offending a policeman, do you?" said Detective Carlyle friendly. "If you stop struggling I'm sure he will let go of you."

Lord Spencer calmed down. Sergeant Thompson got off of him and helped him to his feet. However, he still had a good grasp of his arm just in case Lord Spencer tried to run away.

"Let me introduce myself: I'm Detective Carlyle from the London Police and the gentleman who is making sure you don't try to run away is my colleague Sergeant Thompson."

Übung 31: Übersetzen Sie und enträtseln Sie das Lösungswort!

1. Treppe   ☐ _ _ _ _ _

2. Grab   _ _ _ _ ☐

3. anzeigen   _ _ _ ☐ _ _

4. gut   ☐ _ _ _

5. ankommen   _ _ _ _ _ ☐

6. Kragen   _ _ _ _ ☐ _

7. vorstellen   _ ☐ _ _ _ _ _ _

8. schnell   _ _ _ ☐

Lösung: _ _ _ _ _ _ _ _

Sergeant Thompson tipped his police hat. Lord Spencer looked away in disgust.

"So what do you want from me then? I have not done anything wrong!"

Detective Carlyle's eyebrow went up disapprovingly.

"You are charged with murder!"

"Murder?" Lord Spencer spat the words out. "That is ridiculous!"

The detective ignored this and took out his notebook. He flicked through the pages.

"Is it true you were at the Criterion on Sunday evening?"

Lord Spencer nodded.

"Is it also true you threatened Mr Havisham because you dislike his recently published book?"

"Yes…'dislike' is not quite the right word; I detest it!"

"Do you detest it enough to have murdered him?" asked Detective Carlyle.

"Most certainly not, murder is absolutely against my Christian faith!"

"And what about the death threats?"

"They were just meant to scare him and force Havisham to stop publishing the book. We did not want to kill him."

" '*We*'? Are there more people in on this?"

Übung 32: Welcher Satz enthält die richtige Übersetzung?

1. Die Männer gingen langsam die Treppe hinunter.
   a) ☐ The men gradually walked down the stairs.
   b) ☐ The men slowly walked down the stairs.

2. Er war im Criterion.
   a) ☐ He was on the Criterion.
   b) ☐ He was at the Criterion.

3. Die Polizisten machten sich auf den Weg zurück zur Treppe.
   a) ☐ The policemen headed back to the stairs.
   b) ☐ The policemen directed back to the steps.

4. Lord Spencer beruhigte sich.
   a) ☐ Lord Spencer combed down.
   b) ☐ Lord Spencer calmed down.

5. Lord Spencer verabscheute das Buch.
   a) ☐ Lord Spencer disliked the book.
   b) ☐ Lord Spencer detested the book.

6. Sergeant Thompson licß ihn los.

    a) ☐ Sergeant Thompson let him be.

    b) ☐ Sergeant Thompson let him go.

At this moment Minister Black came hurrying along.

"What is going on here? Let Lord Spencer go at once!" he said angrily.

"I'm afraid that will not be possible, Minister. I'm going to arrest Lord Spencer for the murder of Philip Havisham. To be honest, I should really take you in as well."

The minister laughed out loud. It was not a real laugh, it sounded more like mocking.

"Take me in, what in heavens name for?"

"You lied to us. You have been hiding a murder suspect. For all I know you could be in on the murder, too. I assume the death threats were not just Lord Spencer's idea."

"Okay, I lied and I helped Lord Spencer hide. However, not because he is guilty, but because we knew the police would suspect him. I just wanted to keep him out of the way until the real murderer was found. Anyway, you cannot prove anything!"

Sergeant Thompson smiled triumphantly at his superior.

"Tell him about the cushion, sir."

The minister looked back and forth between the two men.

"Cushion, what cushion?" he asked nervously.

"The murderer used a cushion to silence his gun and the cushion is from Stephan's Hotel."

"I did not take a cushion out of the hotel – I swear!" Lord Spencer protested.

"We'll have to carry on our conversation at the police station, Lord Spencer. Sergeant, if you would kindly escort Lord Spencer to the gate."

"Yes, sir!"

"But you cannot do this!" shouted Minister Black. "I can testify that Lord Spencer came straight to the church right after his quarrel with Mr Havisham."

Übung 33: Welche Synonyme gehören zusammen?

1. hurry
2. honest
3. mock
4. assume
5. murderer
6. conversation
7. quarrel
8. testify
9. angry
10. idea

☐ suggestion
☐ argue
☐ talk
☐ killer
☐ suppose
☐ annoyed
☐ bear witness
☐ truthful
☐ rush
☐ scorn

Detective Carlyle looked at the minister sympathetically.

"I'm afraid you have lied once too often this evening, how am I to believe you now."

"It is true and I also know another ten God-fearing people who will be able to confirm what I told you."

"Did one of these so-called 'God-fearing' persons inform Lord Spencer that Philip Havisham would be dining at the Criterion on Sunday evening?"

"I do not know what you are taking about!"

"We found a note addressed to Lord Spencer telling him where he could find Mr Havisham."

"Somebody slipped the note through my door. Neither the minister nor anybody else from this church has anything to do with it!"

Detective Carlyle sighed.

"Oh, really?" he said in an ironic tone.

The detective tipped his bowler hat.

"Good evening, Minister Black."

The minister was trembling with anger and shook his fist at the policemen.

"This is going to have repercussions, believe me!" Then he said in a more gentle tone: "Don't worry, Manuel; I will get you out of there as fast as I can."

Detective Carlyle walked to the gate where the sergeant was waiting for him. Lord Spencer stood in silence, his head hanging sullenly towards the ground.

Übung 34: Unterstreichen Sie die richtige Alternative!

ÜBUNG 34 !

The (1.) next/after day Detective Carlyle was (2.) called/named into his superior's office. Chief Inspector Gatsby was a very fat man and his face was as grey (3.) like/as the sky on a rainy day. The chief inspector was sitting behind (4.) him/his untidy desk drumming his fingers impatiently on the wood. He was not amused.

"What is this I hear (5.) about/over you locking up Lord Spencer? People, *very important* people have been in and out of my office the whole morning! They all testified that Lord Spencer was with them in the church (6.) whole/all evening."

"But Philip Havisham was murdered in the early evening. He could have killed him and then joined them (7.) at/on the church."

"When was Mr Havisham murdered?"

"Around seven o'clock."

"And at what time did the quarrel between Havisham and Spencer take place?"

"Half past six."

"So we have half an hour between the two incidents."

"Yes, I know that, but…"

Inspector Gatsby did not let him finish his sentence.

"The witnesses testified that Lord Spencer arrived at St Andrews Church at a quarter to seven; meaning that it could not have been him."

! *Übung 35: Schreiben Sie die Uhrzeit aus!*

ÜBUNG 35

1. 06:30 pm *half past six*   6. 17:45 _____

2. 08:00 pm _____   7. 19:35 _____

3. 04:15 am _____   8. 15:50 _____

4. 07:10 pm _____   9. 02:05 pm _____

5. 10:25 am _____   10. 16:20 _____

Detective Carlyle was getting angry. He clenched his fist under the table. Nevertheless, he tried to keep calm.

"But these people are covering for him. They had been sending Havisham death threats and wanted to burn his books publicly. For all I know they could all be in on the murder."

Chief Inspector Gatsby slammed his fist on the table.

"That is outrageous, Detective Carlyle. Do you know who these people are?"

"No, sir, but do tell me," said Detective Carlyle with a smirk on his face.

"I most certainly will not! I don't want you round terrorising innocent citizens. However, the one thing I can tell you is that they are all very respectable and credible citizens of London."

"I can prove Lord Spencer is the murderer. The cushion from the scene of the crime is from the hotel where he lives."

Übung 36: Welche Wörter passen inhaltlich zusammen?

1. hesitate	☐ calm
2. slam	☐ wait
3. burn	☐ door
4. police	☐ crime
5. murder	☐ flame
6. ocean	☐ coach
7. horse	☐ detective

Chief Inspector Gatsby hesitated for a second to think about what Detective Carlyle had said, and then he shook his head.

"Not enough, Carlyle, that is just not enough. Did you find the gun?"

"No, my men searched the church premises and the hotel but they could not find it."

Inspector Gatsby took a deep breath.

"We're letting him go!"

"But…"

"No buts! Go and find the real murderer and leave these innocent people alone."

Detective Carlyle stood up shaking his head. He was about to say something, but changed his mind and headed for the door.

"Good day, sir!"

"I want you to go to Havisham's house. See if you find any clues."

Detective Carlyle did not answer.

"That is an order, Detective!" he shouted after him as he closed the door.

Übung 37: Lesen Sie weiter und ordnen Sie die Buchstaben in Klammern zu sinnvollen Wörtern!

Sergeant Thompson was (1. pmiateityln) _____ waiting for Detective Carlyle outside Inspector Gatsby's office.

"What was all the (2. gnitohus) _____ about?"

"Gatsby wants to let Lord Spencer go (3. refe) _____."

"What? But the evidence against him is (4. vgnilmewhoer) _____."

"I know - that's why I want one of your men to follow him around. Maybe (5. osoern) _____ or later he will give himself away or lead us to the hiding place of the (6. ung) _____."

"Will do, sir! What do we do in the meantime?"

"I guess we should go to Philip Havisham's house or we'll be in big trouble."

"What do you mean?" asked the sergeant puzzled.

Detective Carlyle nodded in the direction of Chief Inspector Gatsby's office.

"Oh, I see!" said Sergeant Thompson and shook his head.

Übung 38: Wählen Sie die richtige Alternative aus!

1. Detective Carlyle was getting _____.
   a) ☐ lucky   b) ☐ angry   c) ☐ happy

2. The note _____ him where to find Mr Havisham
   a) ☐ said   b) ☐ told   c) ☐ claimed

3. The minister was trembling with _____.
   a) ☐ fear   b) ☐ joy   c) ☐ anger

4. Somebody slipped the note _____ Lord Spencer's door.
   a) ☐ through   b) ☐ over   c) ☐ into

5. Chief Inspector Gatsby took a deep _____.
   a) ☐ gasp   b) ☐ breath   c) ☐ pant

6. Lord Spencer was let _____.
   a) ☐ free   b) ☐ in   c) ☐ over

7. Chief Inspector Gatsby _____ his fist on the table.
   a) ☐ smashed   b) ☐ slammed   c) ☐ hammered

Chapter 4: The Man behind the Dandy

Sergeant Thompson whistled. He and Detective Carlyle were standing in the hall of Philip Havisham's house. The doors to the rooms off the hall were wide open: The furniture had been turned upside down; drawers were open and their content hanging out.

"Somebody has certainly turned this house into a pig-sty, sir!" said Sergeant Thompson.

"Yes, I don't think Philip Havisham left his house like this."

"Do you think it was burgled?"

"I'm not quite sure yet. It certainly looks like a burglary, but it is also possible the person was looking for something – maybe something to do with the murder."

"I wonder why nobody has reported this yet. Philip Havisham must have had relatives or at least servants."

"As far as I know he had no living relatives. However, I don't know if he had servants. I think it is best to contact his close friends Simon Manlove, John Pirrip and Stewart Portman. Maybe they can explain why nobody has reported this yet and tell us if something has been stolen."

"I'll get one of my men to contact them."

"Good, Sergeant, in the meantime I'm going to look around the house."

! *Übung 39: Markieren Sie mit richtig ✓ oder falsch – !*

ÜBUNG 39

1. Victorian upper-class people had servants. ☐
2. Philip Havisham had servants. ☐
3. Chief Inspector Gatsby was a very slim man. ☐
4. Philip Havisham's house was burgled. ☐
5. Lord Spencer is the main suspect. ☐
6. The furniture had been toppled onto the street. ☐
7. Philip Havisham's house looked like a horse-stable. ☐

About three quarters of an hour later the sergeant arrived at the house with Philip Havisham's friends. They were all dressed in black as they had just been to Philip Havisham's funeral.

"What has happened here?" cried out Simon Manlove.

"We are not quite sure at the moment, but I thought, gentlemen, you could help us find out," said Detective Carlyle calmly.

The men looked at each other. They all looked very sad. Then John Pirrip looked towards Detective Carlyle.

"With all due respect, Detective, we have just been to Mr Havisham's funeral and are not really up to being questioned just now. Are you sure we can really help you?"

"At least I hope so. What interests me most is why nobody has reported this? Mr Havisham has been dead for nearly three days now."

"Mr Havisham does not have any living relatives", answered Stewart Portman, "but Mr Pirrip has a key and wanted to come and check on things…"

"I just have not been able to make myself do it. There are so many good memories attached to the house," said John Pirrip finishing Stewart Portman's sentence. He sounded very sad.

"I see, and did Philip Havisham not have any servants either?"

The three friends laughed in a soft and rueful way.

"Philip…I mean Mr Havisham hated servants. He believed they were far too inquisitive and corrupt," said Simon Manlove.

The three men smiled and shook their heads. Detective Carlyle waited a few seconds and then said:

"Gentlemen, I would like you to walk around the house with me and tell me if you think anything is missing. I am sure nobody knows this place better than you."

Übung 40: Ordnen Sie das passende Reflexivpronomen zu!

1. I could not make *myself* do it.

2. You could not make _____ do it.

3. He could not make _____ do it.

4. She could not make _____ do it.

ÜBUNG 40

5. It could not make _____ do it.

6. We could not make _____ do it.

7. You could not make _____ do it.

8. They could not make _____ do it.

Together with them, Detective Carlyle looked in every room of the house, but nothing appeared to have been stolen. They all came back down the stairs and stood in the hall by the front door.

"That is strange!" said a perplexed Simon Manlove. "Why should someone break into a place and not steal anything?"

"If I knew that I could solve the case in no time," answered Detective Carlyle. "But I assume the murderer was looking for something."

"For what?" asked John Pirrip.

"I don't know. Maybe he was looking for whatever he killed Mr Havisham for."

The three friends looked even paler and more shocked than in the beginning.

"I think I have strained your nerves enough for today. You may go home now. I will keep you up to date with the investigation."

"Yes, please do so. The sooner you find this terrible murderer the better," Stewart Portman said with a shaky voice.

Philip Havisham's friends shook the policemen's hands, said goodbye and left.

! *Übung 41: Welche Verben und Substantive gehören zusammen?*

ÜBUNG 41

1. solve ☐ a fuss

2. knock ☐ a steak

3. commit ☐ an interview

4. conduct   ☐ a murder

5. eat   ☐ at the door

6. make   ☐ the case

"What shall we do now, sir?" sighed Sergeant Thompson.

"Maybe the murderer has not found what he was looking for. So let's have a look around and see if we can find anything suspicious." Detective Carlyle and Sergeant Thompson began searching Philip Havisham's home. After a while Sergeant Thompson came into Philip Havisham's bedroom. Detective Carlyle's feet were sticking out from under the bed. It had a brass golden bedstead which shone brightly in the summer sun coming through the bedroom window.

Übung 42: Lesen Sie weiter und unterstreichen Sie vier Begriffe, die Erstaunen ausdrücken!

"Find anything, sir?" Sergeant Thompson smirked.

Detective Carlyle's feet wobbled about as he pushed himself back. He surfaced. His hair was quite a mess and he had a very large box in his hand.

"Yes!" he said triumphantly to the sergeant.

The detective laid the box on the bed and opened it. It was full of small black books.

"Diaries!" exclaimed Sergeant Thompson. "What shall we do with them?"

"Read them!" and with this Detective Carlyle gave the sergeant a couple of books.

"Read them?" gasped the sergeant unenthusiastically. "There must be about 40 or 50 in the box!"

"Well, you had better get started then. We don't want to take all day," said Detective Carlyle in a friendly, casual tone.

The sergeant looked baffled.

"If you say so, sir."

He took his share of the diaries and sat on the corner of the bed. Detective Carlyle sat on the other side. After some time the sergeant said: "This chap is unbelievable! Do you know that he had the nerve to con Simon Manlove out of 150 pounds! He wrote here he just did it for pleasure!"

Detective Carlyle shook his head disapprovingly.

"And I just read that he sold two bottles of port to John Pirrip for four times as much as he had paid."

"What was wrong with this man, sir? He betrayed his best friends!"

Sergeant Thompson paused and thought for a second.

"Wait a minute, do you think…"

"No, Sergeant! I don't think that gives a man enough motivation to cold-bloodedly shoot his friend in the heart; even though his behaviour towards them was very shameful. I doubt his friends know of this, but what this information does tell us is that Philip Havisham was not a very honourable man."

"He most certainly wasn't!" said the sergeant in disgust.

Suddenly the doorbell rang.

"I'll answer that," volunteered Sergeant Thompson.

Übung 43: Welche viktorianischen Wörter entsprechen heutigen Ausdrücken?

ÜBUNG 43

1. Sir	☐ talk
2. chap	☐ living-room
3. Madame	☐ guy
4. drawing room	☐ womanizer

5. lady's man   ☐ foyer

6. anteroom   ☐ Mr

7. patter   ☐ Mrs

He went down the stairs and opened the door. Constable Taylor, a young new recruit, was standing in front of the door. He was out of breath.

"Sergeant Thompson, we've just followed Lord Spencer to something which appears to be a hide-out."

"Where is it?"

"Blackwall, on the north bank of the Thames. We followed him to a shed located at the West India Docks."

"Good work, Constable. I will be with you in just a minute."

Sergeant Thompson walked towards the stairs and called to his superior. Detective Carlyle was still reading the diaries when he heard the sergeant's voice: "We have a lead, sir!"

The detective quickly packed the diaries back into the box.

"Very interesting material," he mumbled to himself. "I'll read the rest later."

Übung 44: Setzen Sie die richtige Zukunftsform in die Lücken!

1. We're in a hurry, I'm afraid you _____ have to read the diaries later.

2. Okay, I _____ read them when I get home.

3. This time tomorrow we're _____ know more.

4. I'm _____ read the rest of the diaries tonight.

5. I'm actually _____ get through all of them tonight

   if it's the last thing I ever do.

Detective Carlyle hurried down the stairs with the large box in his hands. The men ran towards the police coach awaiting them at the gate. "Oh, I nearly forgot to tell you that Dr Brown has identified the bullet which belongs to the murder weapon: Havisham was killed with a Remington Revolver," Constable Taylor panted.

"Just as I thought! Maybe Lord Spencer has led us to its hiding place."

They hastily climbed into the coach, the coachman cracked his whip and the coach shot off.

! ÜBUNG 45

Übung 45: Was ist gemeint? Setzen Sie ein!
(hide-out, diary, bedroom, murder weapon, constable, volunteer, a mess)

1. a book to document appointments: _____

2. a remote hiding place: _____

3. a place to sleep in: _____

4. lowest police rank: _____

5. to do something of free will: _____

6. something someone is killed with: _____

7. in a very bad condition: _____

Detective Carlyle, Sergeant Thompson and Constable Taylor approached two other policemen. They were hiding behind an old dock container and were observing the shed which was close to the water.

"Is he still in there?" asked Detective Carlyle.

"Yes, sir!" answered one of the constables. "I wonder what he has been doing all this time."

"We'll soon find out. I'll count to three and then we'll sneak over, but be careful, the suspect could be armed."

The policemen moved carefully towards the shed keeping their heads down low. As they reached the shed they crouched down. Detective Carlyle carefully looked into one of the windows. What he saw surprised him. His eyebrow went up.

"Looks like a game of whist!" he said astonished.

"Whist, sir?!" asked Sergeant Thompson.

Everybody looked puzzled.

"Yes, Lord Spencer is sitting in there with three other men. I think I've seen one of them before, I just can't remember where."

"What shall we do?"

"I say we take them in. Unofficial gambling is against the law!"

"I'll count to three again and then I want two of your men to kick the door down…one…two…three…"

Two constables kicked the door down and blew their whistles.

"The game is over!" they cried.

They were followed by the sergeant and the detective. There was a lot of turmoil.

Übung 46: Setzen Sie die passende Mengenbezeichnung ein!
(a lot of, much)

1. The case is not solved yet. There still are _____ things to be done.

2. Lord Spencer is in _____ trouble.

3. Detective Carlyle asked _____ questions.

4. But he did not really have very _____ time.

5. Lord Spencer did not say very _____.

One of the men tried to escape, but he was quickly caught by a young and swift constable. Lord Spencer looked surprised.

"Detective Carlyle, I had hoped I had seen the last of you. Did Chief Inspector Gatsby not give you orders to leave me alone?"

"Chief Inspector Gatsby believes you are innocent, but I don't." Detective Carlyle turned to the two constables. "Search the hut and Lord Spencer for the gun, please!"

The policemen went to work.

Lord Spencer smiled mockingly.

"I have no gun, why do you not believe me?"

"Gun? What gun?" one of the gamblers asked Lord Spencer nervously.

He was a very well-dressed man, as were all of the gentlemen present.

*Übung 47: Vervollständigen Sie die Sätze mit **good** oder **well**!*

ÜBUNG 47

1. Detective Carlyle is a very _____ policeman.

2. Sergeant Thompson does his job really _____.

3. Lord Spencer appears to be _____ at lying.

4. Sir James is a _____ whist player.

5. All of the gentlemen were very _____ dressed.

6. Some people are just _____ for nothing.

7. Just as _____ Detective Carlyle caught them gambling.

"Nothing to worry about, Sir James. It's just some kind of mis-understanding," said Lord Spencer.

"I bloody well hope so!" he said angrily. "Bad enough them catching us here playing a game of whist. If this is made public…"

"…Nobody is going to make anything public!" interrupted the man Detective Carlyle thought he knew from somewhere.

"I think that is up to me to decide, Mr…," Detective Carlyle made a gesture for the man to finish his sentence.

"*Lord* Fellowes!" he said in a threatening tone.

"Lord Fellowes? I am sure that rings a bell."

"I most certainly would hope so. I am First Lord of the Admiralty – as you know a very high position in the British Parliament."

Lord Fellowes paused to let his great words sink in. Detective Carlyle looked at him pensively and sighed. He knew what he was about to do could get him into great trouble with his superior.

"Lord Fellowes, gentlemen – I am afraid I will have to arrest you for illegal gambling."

There was uproar in the shed. The constables started taking the men outside. They protested loudly. Constable Taylor came over to Detective Carlyle.

"I'm afraid we could not find the gun."

"Never mind, I'm sure we'll find it sooner or later."

Just at that moment Lord Fellowes was being escorted out. He gave Detective Carlyle a very angry look.

"You will pay for this!" he shouted.

"I know, I know!" said Detective Carlyle with a distinctly gloomy tone to his voice.

! *Übung 48: Welches Wort ist das „schwarze Schaf"?*

1. find, discover, ascertain, mislay
2. hope, crave, dread, anticipate
3. worry, fret, exasperate, wish
4. right, wrong, incorrect, false
5. innocent, guilty, guiltless, blameless
6. believe, trust, doubt, rely
7. hide, reveal, conceal, mask
8. angry, fuming, glad, furious

The last man to be taken out of the shed was Lord Spencer. His seeming confidence had disappeared. He was feeling very sorry for himself. He looked sadly at Detective Carlyle.

"You caught me gambling, but that does not mean I am a murderer. I want to be honest with you: I am addicted to gambling. Why do you think I live in such a poor hotel? It is because I waste all of my money on gambling."

Detective Carlyle looked him straight in the eye. For some reason his police-instinct was telling him to believe Lord Spencer.

"Is that how you ended up in the hands of that religious fanatic Minister Black?"

"Yes, I was looking for spiritual guidance. I had really wanted to stop. It is not much of a life you know, losing all your money at a silly game."

Tears welled up in Lord Spencer's eyes. He was very embarrassed by this and quickly wiped them away. Detective Carlyle looked at him sympathetically.

"Well, by the looks of it the Minister seems to have got you into even more trouble and he has apparently not been able to help you fight your addiction either."

"I had stopped for a while", Lord Spencer insisted, "however, after all the trouble you caused me, accusing me of murder and all that, I started to gamble again."

"I am sorry to hear that, but a lot of the evidence does seem to make you appear guilty. We will just have to wait and see how the further investigations turn out."

Detective Carlyle nodded in the direction of the exit. The constable escorted Lord Spencer out of the shed.

*Übung 49: Mit oder ohne Artikel? Setzen Sie, wenn nötig, **the** ein!*

1. They were walking in _____ same direction.

2. Such is _____ life.

3. Lord Spencer got out of _____ bed early to play cards.

4. Lord Spencer liked to go to _____ church.

5. Sir James knows a lot about _____ history of England.

6. _____ life Mister Black leads is very boring.

ÜBUNG 49

"So what do you think, sir; do you believe him?"

"He seems to be telling the truth. If he isn't he sure is a very good liar. What does seem plausible to me is that my long experience with the police has taught me that someone with a gambling addiction would not break into a house with so many riches as Havisham's and resist stealing something."

"You do have a point. Do you think someone has tried to set Lord Spencer up?"

"It is a possibility. Lord Spencer was easy bait as he detested Philip Havisham's book. He was probably just waiting for a chance to confront him."

"So maybe the poor man just walked right into a trap?"

"Yes, it's possible. The person who allegedly passed the note through his door could easily have taken a cushion from the hotel; leading us straight to Lord Spencer."

The detective and the sergeant walked slowly towards the police coach.

"I think we've had enough excitement for today. It's time we went home; I've still got those diaries to read through. Who knows, maybe I'll find something that might help us solve this most puzzling case."

Übung 50: Welche Bedeutung haben folgende Sätze?

1. Lord Spencer was looking for spiritual guidance.
   a) ☐ Lord Spencer needed more fun.
   b) ☐ Lord Spencer needed a drink.
   c) ☐ Lord Spencer needed help.

2. Minister Black is a religious fanatic.
   a) ☐ Minister Black is narrow-minded.
   b) ☐ Minister Black is open-minded.
   c) ☐ Minister Black is immoral.

3. He walked into a trap.
   a) ☐ He got lost.
   b) ☐ He got caught.
   c) ☐ He got hit.

4. Detective Carlyle was sympathetic.
  a) ☐ Detective Carlyle was a nice person.
  b) ☐ Detective Carlyle was considerate.
  c) ☐ Detective Carlyle disapproved.

5. Lord Spencer appears to be guilty.
  a) ☐ Lord Spencer is unlikely to be guilty.
  b) ☐ Lord Spencer admitted he was guilty.
  c) ☐ Lord Spencer is probably guilty.

Chapter 5: The Beautiful Baroness McKee

Detective Carlyle and Sergeant Thompson met early at the police station the next day. The two policemen sat themselves down in Detective Carlyle's office. They had steaming cups of tea in front of them. The detective had not slept much, but reading all of Philip Havisham's diaries had been worth staying up most of the night.

"What did you find out, sir?" asked Sergeant Thompson trying to hide his excitement.

"Philip Havisham had a relationship with a woman named Baroness McKee."

The sergeant looked disappointed.

"If you will excuse me saying so – but that's not really very surprising, sir; the man had a few affairs in his time!"

Detective Carlyle smiled wisely at Sergeant Thompson and lent back on his chair.

"Let me finish, Sergeant. As St Augustine said: 'Patience is the companion of wisdom'."

Sergeant Thompson looked like a school boy who had been told off by his teacher.

"Sorry, sir – I'm just very curious!"

"Indeed you are, and that is a quality a job like ours needs."

Detective Carlyle tipped his nose with his finger.

"Anyway, Baroness McKee must be a very beautiful woman; in fact the most beautiful woman in London, if we want to believe Philip Havisham – and I guess, as we know by now, the man knew what he was talking about."

Sergeant Thompson chuckled.

"But the thing about Baroness McKee was", Detective Carlyle carried on, "that she was not interested in Philip Havisham in the least – she was a very conservative Lady and did not like Mr Havisham's way of life."

"So what made her change her mind?" asked Sergeant Thompson impatiently.

! *Übung 51: Ordnen Sie die Wörter auf der rechten Seite den Begriffen auf der linken zu!*

1. gasp
2. wisdom
3. guess
4. life
5. needs
6. bait
7. manage
8. pretend
9. believe
10. uproar

a) ☐ handle, cope, run
b) ☐ lure, attract, tempt
c) ☐ wants, requirements, desires
d) ☐ consider, think, trust
e) ☐ pant, puff, breath
f) ☐ make-up, play, make-believe
g) ☐ presume, assume, estimate
h) ☐ mayhem, upheaval, turmoil
i) ☐ being, existence, mortal
k) ☐ insight, understand, knowledge

Detective Carlyle's bushy red eyebrow went up disapprovingly. This gesture silenced Sergeant Thompson.

"She changed her mind because he managed to make her believe he was a new person; for weeks he played the perfect gentleman and pretended to be a newborn man. In the end he eventually won her heart."

"That is unbelievable, sir!" gasped Sergeant Thompson. "Philip Havisham was a very devious man!"

"It gets worse," said Detective Carlyle grimly.

"How much worse can it get?"

"Well, he did all of it because of a bet…"

"A bet?" Sergeant Thompson could not believe his ears.

"Yes, he bet with a friend he could win her heart."

"But that means he did not really care about her. The only thing that really attracted him was that she was hard to get."

"I assume so."

"That is outrageous!"

Übung 52: Enträtseln Sie die fünf Begriffe, die man stellvertretend für **outrageous** *sagen könnte!*

1. lufemsha _____	4. ablepicdes _____
2. kingoshc _____	5. ppallniga _____
3. racegulfsid _____	

!

ÜBUNG 52

Detective Carlyle nodded with a sigh.

"It certainly is, Sergeant."

"What happened after he won her heart?"

"He broke it."

"What did he do – just left her and that was it?"

"Yes!"

"But a woman of her rank and moral integrity must have been shattered!"

Sergeant Thompson paused and thought for a moment.

"She definitely has a motive," he remarked.

"She sure has, but the question is if a lady of such integrity could really cold-bloodedly murder another person?"

"But Philip Havisham did treat Baroness McKee very badly and hurt her to a great extent – the lies, deceit and dishonesty she experienced were terrible!"

"Exactly! That is why I think we should pay Baroness McKee a visit."

The two policemen took a last sip of their tea and left the office.

Übung 53: Bilden Sie sinnvolle Sätze!

ÜBUNG 53

1. relationship Baroness he McKee woman a with called a had

_____

2. had cups front in steaming they them of tea of

_____

3. place more fortress if looks ask you me this like a

_____

4. left he her won after heart he her

_____

5. really could Baroness McKee murder person a

_____

6. is Philip Havisham man devious a

_____

7. share took of sat corner at bed of diaries a he the the and the

_____

8. Thompson Sergeant read want books did not to the

Detective Carlyle and Sergeant Thompson arrived at Baroness McKee's house. It was extremely large and located in Mayfair – a very aristocratic district. The crème de la crème of Victorian London's high-society lived there. A long, high iron fence protected the property from unwanted visitors. Each bar was spear-shaped and looked very sharp. Sergeant Thompson looked bewildered.

"That place looks more like a fortress than a house, if you ask me!"

"Yes, but it still couldn't protect the baroness from Philip Havisham," Detective Carlyle remarked.

The policemen got out of the coach and climbed the steps to the doorway bridge which led over a six foot deep ditch on either side. Sergeant Thompson opened the small gate at the top of the steps and let his superior pass. Detective Carlyle used the knocker – an iron loop-shaped device which hung on the door. Shortly afterwards a butler opened the door.

Übung 54: Lesen Sie weiter und setzen Sie das passende Wort ein! (wish, home, investigating, unnoticeable, luck, message, statue, observed, contact)

"You (1.) _____?" he asked in a monotonous and almost bored tone. "Who may I announce?"

"My name is Detective Carlyle from the London Police. I wish to speak to Baroness McKee. It is very important; I am (2.) _____ the murder of Philip Havisham."

The detective (3.) _____ a slight twinge at the corner of the butler's mouth. Apart from this almost (4.) _____ movement, the butler's face did not alter – it reminded the detective of a (5.) _____ made of stone

"I am afraid Baroness McKee is not at (6.) _____ at the moment. Do you wish to leave a (7.) _____?"

"Could you please tell her I was here and that I would be very grateful if she would (8.) _____ me as soon as possible."

"I will most certainly do so," replied the butler and closed the door.

Sergeant Thompson shrugged:

"No (9.) _____, eh?"

The policeman turned away from the door. In that moment Detective Carlyle glanced sideways to the window at the front of the house. He saw a curtain move slightly. He looked away as if nothing had happened.

"I wouldn't say that," he mumbled to himself while they walked back down the stairs.

Detective Carlyle and Sergeant Thompson got back into the coach. As soon as it turned the corner Detective Carlyle asked the coachman to stop.

"Why are we stopping, sir?" asked Sergeant Thompson puzzled.

"Because Baroness McKee is probably at home."

"How do you know?"

"I saw a curtain move in one of her windows. I assume she was watching us, to see who we were."

Sergeant Thompson was impressed. He smiled at his superior and tipped his nose with his finger. Detective Carlyle smiled back. The men got out of the coach and walked back to the entrance of the street where Baroness McKee's house was. There was a wall they could hide behind allowing them to observe the baroness's home.

"What are we going to do now, sir?"

"I suggest we wait and see what happens. She might leave the house sooner or later. Then we'll follow her."

Übung 55: Unterstreichen und verbessern Sie im folgenden Textabschnitt die sieben falsch geschriebenen Wörter!

After one and a half hours stil nothing had happened. Sergeant Thompson was getting impatient.

"Maybe she isn't at home after all," he said.

Detective Carlyle gave his sergeant another one of his disapproving looks.

"I know, I know: 'Patience is the companion of wissdom'!" he said in a slightly irritated tone.

All of a suden the baroness's front door opened and an astonishingly beautiful and elegant woman appeared. Sergeant Thompson was speechless. He just watched her descend the steps in amazement. Detective Carlyle looked to the side and observed the open-mouthed sergeant.

"Sergeant Thompson?" he said amuced.

"Sir?" said the sergeant without taking his eyes off the baroness. His voice had a distracted and remot ring to it.

"We have work to do?"

"Oh…yes…of course…you are absolutely right!" replied the sergeant as if he had just been awoken from a beautiful dreem.

The policemen started to follow Baroness McKee. They followed her to the neighbourhood of Berkley Square.

"I don't think such a beautiful lady could just have walked in and out of the Criterion Restaurant without being noticed, do you?" Sergeant Thompson asked Detective Carlyle.

"No, I don't, but she could have disguised herself or perhaps she paid someone to kill Philip Havisham."

Sergeant Thompson looked at Detective Carlyle in disbelief.

"I think she is innocent. I mean, she must be…such an attractive and delicate-looking being…she probably couldn't hurt a fly!"

"Time will tell, Romeo!" laughed Detective Carlyle.

1. _____   5. _____

2. _____   6. _____

3. _____   7. _____

4. _____

Sergeant Thompson looked a little embarrassed and went red.

Just off Berkley Square Baroness McKee entered a café. The policemen waited on the other side of the road. They could see what she was doing through the large glass window. She greeted a man with a nod and sat down at his table. He was well-dressed, however, he had a cruel and rough-looking face, which did not seem to match his exquisite and expensive outfit.

"Don't seem to be the best of friends," said Detective Carlyle.

"Wait a minute, I know that man from somewhere!" exclaimed Sergeant Thompson. "Well, I'll be damned, that's William Butcher!"

"William Butcher? That man has been in and out of jail more times than the prison director himself!"

"You can say that again. He has worked through the catalogue of offences like others through a restaurant menu: assault, dealing with opium and many other offences – you name it, he's done it."

"Murder?"

"I'm not quite sure about murder, sir. What I want to know is why in heavens name Baroness McKee keeps such bad company!"

"Maybe our baroness is not as innocent as she looks."

Sergeant Thompson was about to protest when she suddenly passed an envelope under the table to William Butcher.

"What do you think is in the envelope?" asked Sergeant Thompson.

"I'm not quite sure, certainly not any good news. As soon as William Butcher leaves the café, we'll follow him and wait for the right moment to get a hold of him."

"And what about the baroness?"

"We'll leave her for just now. I don't want her to know we are on to her quite yet."

Übung 56: Welche Bedeutung haben die Sätze? Kreuzen Sie an!

1. Well, I'll be damned!
   a) ☐ That really surprises me.
   b) ☐ I am going to hell.
   c) ☐ The water pressure is high.

2. He has been in and out of jail more times than the director himself.
   a) ☐ He is more important than the jail director.
   b) ☐ He has been in jail very often.
   c) ☐ He likes going to jail very much.

3. He has worked through the catalogue of offences like others through a restaurant menu.
   a) ☐ He likes good food.
   b) ☐ He likes to read.
   c) ☐ He has a long criminal record.

4. You name it, he's done it!
   a) ☐ He will do anything you say.
   b) ☐ There is not a crime he has not committed.
   c) ☐ He has great knowledge of things.

5. She is in bad company.
   a) ☐ She is with someone or people, who are dangerous.
   b) ☐ She works for a terrible firm.
   c) ☐ She dislikes good company.

Shortly after, both the baroness and William Butcher left the café. The policemen followed William Butcher for a while. The criminal had no idea he was being followed. He turned into a small narrow lane.

"Let's try and get ahold of him now."

Sergeant Thompson and Detective Carlyle ran into the lane after William Butcher. He heard the steps and turned around, the policemen were very close. The criminal took to his feet. Sergeant Thompson finally caught up with him. Detective Carlyle was still a bit further behind. The sergeant held William Butcher by his collar and pushed him against the wall. William Butcher did not move and did not say a thing. He seemed very calm.

"Now, no funny tricks!" said Sergeant Thompson.

William Butcher just smiled mockingly. His smile looked creepy because his front teeth were missing. Sergeant Thompson put his

hand into the inside pocket of William Butcher's jacket and took out the envelope.

"So what have we got here?" said Sergeant Thompson triumphantly. At that moment Detective Carlyle arrived. He was breathing heavily. The sergeant turned around and handed the envelope to his superior. William Butcher used this moment of distraction to his advantage. He punched Sergeant Thompson in the stomach and pushed him away. The blow was very hard and the sergeant toppled over. William Butcher ran as fast as he could. Sergeant Thompson got back on his feet.

"Come back, you scoundrel!" he shouted in anger and started to run after him, but William Butcher managed to escape.

Übung 57: Füllen Sie die Lücken mit dem passenden Wort!
(under, used, about, down 2x, at, up, behind, to 2x)

1. Philip Havisham worked _____ the menu.

2. Lord Spencer was _____ to protest.

3. The policemen started _____ follow him.

4. She passed the envelope _____ the table.

5. Detective Carlyle _____ the door knocker.

6. The baroness was not _____ home.

7. The policemen crouched _____ .

8. They finally caught _____ with him.

9. William Butcher took _____ his feet.

10. Sergeant Thompson hid _____ a wall.

"Are you all right, Sergeant?" asked Detective Carlyle as the former returned back to the lane.

Thompson was holding his stomach and was out of breath.

"Yes, but if I ever catch that man he will be sorry!"

"I'm sure we'll get him sooner or later," said Detective Carlyle.

"So what's in the envelope?" asked Sergeant Thompson as he leaned against the wall still puffing and panting.

"Money – a lot of money!"

Detective Carlyle waved a bundle of notes in the air.

"I hate to ask this: Do you think the baroness paid him to kill Philip Havisham?"

"It's possible, Or can you think of any other reason why she met up with such a person and gave him a lot of money?"

Sergeant Thompson shook his head.

"Well, let's get back to her house and I won't let her arrogant butler blow us off this time."

Übung 58: Setzen Sie im folgenden Text die richtigen Fragepronomen ein!

(whose, whose, who, who, which, what, where)

1. _____ is Baroness McKee?

2. _____ did she meet William Butcher?

3. _____ money was in the envelope?

4. In _____ café did Baroness McKee and William Butcher meet?

5. _____ is the name of the square in which Philip Havisham's house is located?

6. _____ is the main murder suspect?

7. _____ servant opened the door?

Detective Carlyle knocked at the baroness's door. The butler opened the door.

"Oh, it is you again!" he said in his arrogant tone. "I told you the baroness is not in at the moment."

Sergeant Thompson shot forward.

"Now listen, you. I've had enough of your nonsense! We know the baroness is at home, now let us in!" he said angrily.

The butler's mouth twitched again. Detective Carlyle gave his sergeant a slight, calming push to the side.

"I'll deal with this, Sergeant."

He looked the butler straight in the eye.

"We have reason to believe that Baroness McKee is involved in the murder of Philip Havisham. Just tell her we followed her to the Café Royal and let her make up her own mind whether or not she wants to talk to us after all."

The butler disappeared without a word and came back to the door shortly afterwards. He let the policemen in – his face showing a slight look of disgust.

"Thank you!" said Detective Carlyle triumphantly and lifted his bowler hat in a greeting gesture. Sergeant Thompson gave the butler an angry look. The butler did not seem to care – he did not look at the policemen once and stared straight ahead in the direction of the wall. He closed the door.

"If you will kindly follow me," he said and walked down the long, bright hall in front of the policemen. Sergeant Thompson could not hide that he was impressed by the thick red carpet, the paintings of long dead ancestors and the gold framed mirrors, which decorated

the hallway. The corridor seemed to be endless until they eventually reached a door – the butler opened it and entered the room. Detective Carlyle and Sergeant Thompson could not get a proper look of the inside because the butler had only left the door half open.

"Madame, the two gentlemen from the police I told you about."

"Yes, let them in," a soft female voice answered.

Übung 59: Übersetzen Sie!

1. Die Baronin hatte eine geheimnisvolle Ausstrahlung.

_____

2. Sie konnten nicht richtig in das Zimmer sehen.

_____

3. Sergeant Thompson griff in seine Innentasche.

_____

4. Sobald William Butcher das Café verlässt, werden wir ihm folgen.

_____

5. Die Polizisten näherten sich vorsichtig den Kisten.

_____

6. Detective Carlyle sah, dass der Vorhang sich bewegte.

_____

The doors opened and the policemen stepped into a large drawing room. The baroness lay on a chaise longue – a couch in the shape of a chair. She was leaning gracefully against the sofa's arm supporting her head with her hand. She looked almost like a Roman empress. The chaise longue was covered in white satin and in front of it was a huge Persian rug. The butler bowed, left the drawing room, closing the doors behind him.

"How may I help you, Gentlemen?" asked the baroness. There was something about her voice that did not seem right. It sounded slow and drowsy. Detective Carlyle and Sergeant Thompson looked at each other.

"I am Detective Carlyle and this is my colleague Sergeant Thompson – we are from the London Police," the detective said with his most formal voice.

Baroness McKee glanced at Sergeant Thompson standing in his police uniform.

"Well, that would be hard to guess!" she said in a dry, sarcastic tone. "So what does the London Police want from me?"

Detective Carlyle cleared his throat. The baroness exuded a bizarre, secretive aura and her beauty combined with her aristocratic self-confidence had a disarming effect on both policemen.

"We are investigating the murder of Philip Havisham – he was shot dead a few days ago in the Criterion."

"Yes, I have heard of that. What a shame," said Baroness McKee sarcastically.

Detective Carlyle cleared his throat again.

"Well, what I would like to know is where you were on Sunday the 6th of July."

The baroness laughed. It was a loud, almost hysterical laugh. The policemen exchanged looks again. Sergeant Thompson shrugged helplessly.

Übung 60: Lesen Sie weiter und unterstreichen Sie im Text die Synonyme der Wörter in Klammern!
(1. condemning, 2. lack discretion, 3. did you find that out,
4. that is typical of him, 5. assume)

"Where I was? You are not really accusing me of the murder, Detective Carlyle?"

"To be honest, Madame, we do have reason to suspect you."

"And what may that be?" she asked coldly.

"I do not want to be indiscreet, but we know you had a relationship with Mr Havisham…"

"…But you *are* being indiscreet," interrupted Baroness McKee angrily. "How did you find out about this? And if it is true, how does that make me a murder suspect?"

"We also know that Mr Havisham treated you…how shall I say…very badly."

This time the baroness laughed hysterically.

"Badly? I like that, I like that very much! Very good, Detective, very good!" Then she all of a sudden stopped laughing. Her face became very serious. "Now, how do you know of this?" she asked grimly.

"Mr Havisham wrote diaries, I read about it in one of them."

"Trust him!" sighed Baroness McKee. "And now you believe I shot him because of all he did to me."

"Yes!"

"Well, I wish I had, but I must disappoint you, I did not."

"That could be true, however, we have reason to believe you paid William Butcher to kill him. We saw you meeting him at the Café Royal," said Sergeant Thompson.

"Yes, I know you know that, but what does that prove?" asked the baroness impatiently. "For all you know he could be my new fiancé

– I seem to have been quite keen on dishonest men lately," she chuckled.

Detective Carlyle tried to ignore this remark. He was beginning to feel very sorry for Baroness McKee. She seemed to be in great emotional distress.

"Why did you pay him so much money then?"

Baroness McKee looked at the policemen. She seemed to be thinking hard about something. For a few seconds there was nothing but silence in the room. Then the baroness moved into a sitting position. In the process of this she nearly lost her balance. Sergeant Thompson was about to hurry over and catch her, but she managed to stabilize herself.

"I take opium! I take it because it is the only thing on earth that helps me forget what Philip Havisham did to me."

Detective Carlyle and Sergeant Thompson looked a little embarrassed.

Übung 61: Welches Wort ist das „schwarze Schaf"?

1. dishonest, good-natured, deceitful, devious
2. meet, gather, leave, congregate
3. mention, remark, unspoken, say
4. money, riches, penniless, wealthy
5. book, newspaper, novel, sign
6. letter, stamp, address, account
7. evening, breakfast, morning, afternoon
8. week, month, age, year

"I meet William Butcher every two weeks at the Café Royal and pay him for his deliveries – he sells me opium! I am not sorry in the least that Philip Havisham is dead, however, believe me I did not kill him."

"Why did you meet with him yourself? You could have sent one of your servants."

"I never send a servant. I want to keep my problem as secret as possible – you know how much people gossip nowadays."

Baroness McKee laid her head in her hands and began to sob.

Sergeant Thompson looked helplessly across to his superior.

"So what do you think?" he whispered.

"I believe her," Detective Carlyle whispered back. "But I still want one of your men to find William Butcher and question him – see if he has an alibi for Sunday evening."

"What shall we do about…?" Sergeant Thompson nodded in the direction of the baroness.

"I think its best just to go and leave the poor woman alone."

Detective Carlyle looked over at the baroness. She had not moved. He shook his head, feeling very sorry for her. Then he turned around and walked towards the door.

"We can't just leave her like this!" Sergeant Thompson whispered.

"I'm afraid there is nothing we can do! It would be very indiscreet to do anything else," replied the detective and walked on.

Sergeant Thompson looked at Baroness McKee and then looked towards his superior. He was not quite sure what to do. He eventually decided to follow his superior.

ÜBUNG 62

Übung 62: Finden Sie die weibliche Entsprechung für die männlichen Adelstitel!

1. Baron _____   4. Viscount _____

2. Lord _____   5. Duke _____

3. King _____   6. Prince _____

Detective Carlyle and Sergeant Thompson stood in front of the baroness's house. The sergeant was pale.

"Where do we go from here, sir?" he asked a little weary, looking at the detective.

"Well, we don't have much. If Baroness McKee really had nothing to do with the murder then all we know is that whoever killed Philip Havisham must have had it well planned. We also know the murderer was looking for something in his house."

"What could it be?"

"I don't know – possibly something worth killing a man for. Let's go back to Havisham's house – perhaps we overlooked something the first time. That gives us at least something to do until William Butcher has been questioned."

Übung 63: Welche Relativpronomen gehören in die Lücken? Vervollständigen Sie die Sätze!
(who, who's, that, whose, which)

1. Baroness McKee's fiancé, _____ from London, was a very devious man.

2. Sergeant Thompson _____ truncheon fell on his foot felt great agony.

3. The house _____ the policemen went to was like a fortress.

4. Dandies _____ treat women badly should be sent to jail.

5. The Criterion, _____ usually opens on a Sunday evening, was closed.

Chapter 6: Who is Miss SW?

Just as Detective Carlyle and Sergeant Thompson were walking across Grosvenor Square to Philip Havisham's house they met John Pirrip. He smiled when he saw the policemen.

"Detective Carlyle, Sergeant Thompson, what a pleasure to meet you here," he said casually.

"Good day, Mr Pirrip – on your way to the Music Academy?" asked Detective Carlyle. John Pirrip looked surprised. Detective Carlyle pointed at the violin case and smiled.

"Oh, yes of course. I thought there for a minute you could read my mind, Detective."

"If I could read minds, Mr Pirrip, I would solve every police case in no time," chuckled Detective Carlyle.

"Are you on your way to Mr Havisham's house?" asked John Pirrip in a more serious tone.

"In fact we are," answered Detective Carlyle.

"Are you making any progress in the murder investigation?"

"We have a few leads, however, nothing we can talk about at the moment."

"That I understand, Detective Carlyle. Well then, I have got to hurry, my class starts soon, please keep me informed."

The men said goodbye to each other and went their separate ways.

3. sen. _____

4. GB _____

5. ca. _____

6. BC _____

As soon as the policemen entered Philip Havisham's house, Detective Carlyle checked the inside of the drawing room door.

"What are you doing, sir?" asked Sergeant Thompson puzzled.

Detective Carlyle smiled triumphantly.

"It's gone!"

"What has gone?"

"My hair!"

"Your hair? You still have *all* your hair, if you ask me!" exclaimed a perplexed Sergeant Thompson.

"No, no!" said the detective laughing. "I used an old police trick: I stuck one of my hairs between the door's wooden frames."

"Why did you do that?"

"So that I could tell if somebody had been here and had opened the door."

"Oh, and now it's gone?" said the sergeant who was beginning to understand what was going on.

"Exactly – this probably proves that the murderer returned; meaning he had not found what he was looking for the first time!"

"That would mean there was or still is something in the house which is connected in some way to the murder."

"Yes, and if it's still here we're going to find it this time. Let's start looking, Sergeant. We must be more accurate. Don't leave anything out. Look behind pictures; search for loose panels and floorboards."

! *Übung 65: Übersetzen Sie und enträtseln Sie das zusammengesetzte Lösungswort!*

1. Minute   _ _ _ ☐ _ _
2. Fortschritte   ☐ _ _ _ _ _ _ _
3. blass   ☐ _ _ _
4. verblüfft   _ ☐ _ _ _ _ _ _
5. verstehen   _ _ _ _ ☐ _ _ _ _ _
6. kichern   _ _ _ ☐ _ _ _
7. Eifersucht   _ _ _ ☐ _ _ _ _
8. eifrig   _ ☐ _ _ _
9. Opfer (Plural)   _ _ _ _ _ _ ☐
10. Fall   _ _ ☐ _

Lösung: _ _ _ _ _ - _ _ _ _ _

The policemen began their searching. Sergeant Thompson worked his way down the hall. He lifted back every picture and knocked against the wall to check if it was hollow. The sergeant was just getting to the last picture when he saw something lying on the floor. He went to see what it was and discovered a wallet. Sergeant Thompson picked it up and opened it. He whistled. There was a name on the inside. It read: Manuel Spencer. He hurried with it to the kitchen and found Detective Carlyle on his hands and knees trying to pull up a loose wooden plank.

"Oh, Sergeant, you're just in time, come and help me with this, please."

"Sir, look what I found!" Sergeant Thomson exclaimed and gave Detective Carlyle the wallet. "It belongs to Lord Spencer!"

Detective Carlyle inspected it and scratched his head thoughtfully.

"This seems to prove he was in the house. He probably dropped the wallet by accident."

"So he is the murderer after all!"

"The evidence is certainly overwhelming. Funny though, I believed the chap. My instinct doesn't usually let me down," wondered Detective Carlyle.

"Maybe you're getting old!" joked Sergeant Thompson.

Detective Carlyle did not laugh. He gave the sergeant a disapproving look.

"Sorry, sir, it was just a joke! I was getting a little exited about solving the case."

"I wouldn't quite call it solved yet. There are still many questions to be answered. For example: What is under this loose floorboard. Would you be so kind and help me pull it up?"

Übung 66: Beantworten Sie die Fragen zum Text!

1. What were Detective Carlyle and Sergeant Thompson doing when they met John Pirrip?

_____

2. What did John Pirrip think Detective Carlyle could do?

_____

3. Whose wallet did Sergeant Thompson find?

_____

4. Why is John Pirrip in a hurry?

_____

5. What did Detective Carlyle do with one of his hairs?

_____

6. Where did Sergeant Thompson find Detective Carlyle?

_____

7. What was Detective Carlyle doing as Sergeant Thompson entered the kitchen?

_____

Sergeant Thompson knelt down beside Detective Carlyle and helped him loosen the floorboard. The men pulled it up and found a bundle of letters underneath. Detective Carlyle removed them.

"This fellow Havisham sure liked to write," stated Sergeant Thompson.

"Let's see if the letters are actually written by Havisham first before we jump to any conclusions."

Detective Carlyle opened an envelope and looked at it. He opened another and then another.

"They're not written by him; they appear to be from someone with the initials SW."

"SW? Who could that be?"

"I don't know, but they seem to be love letters."

Detective Carlyle read a part of one out aloud:

"…Why do you not want me to leave him? We could be so happy together. I don't care what the others say as long as I can be with you…"

The detective picked up another letter and read from it:

"…Oh, please do not reject me like this. You said you loved me and we would be together for ever. If it has anything to do with him, I promise you he means nothing to me…"

Übung 67: Lesen Sie weiter und unterstreichen Sie die richtige Alternative!

"Do none of the letters (1.) say/tell who her fiancé is?" asked Sergeant Thompson.

"No, she always addresses (2.) him/his as 'he' or 'him'."

Detective Carlyle opened another envelope and began to read aloud:

"…I am pregnant and very sure the child is (3.) yours/your's. I am going to leave him and come to you. This child is definitely a sign that we belong together…"

Sergeant Thompson looked shocked.

"I don't like the sound of (4.) when/where this story is going," he said and started to read a new letter:

"…An abortion…how dare you propose such a terrible thing…once you said you loved me…we need to talk, I suggest we (5.) meat/meet at our special meeting-place, Vauxhall Bridge."

Sergeant Thompson's hands were shaking.

"Well, if that man wasn't dead I would certainly kill him!" he said in an angry voice. "He must have been the reincarnation of the Devil!"

"Now, now, Sergeant Thompson; don't get carried away (6.) by/with your emotions. I don't like what we have found out (7.) on/about Havisham either, but we have got to stay professional," said Detective Carlyle firmly.

Sergeant Thompson took a deep breath and tried to calm down:

"Do you think SW could have been or even still is Lord Spencer's fiancée and he found out about the affair?"

"Maybe, we'll need to find that out. That would mean he killed Philip Havisham more out of jealousy than because of his book, or perhaps because of both."

"There is one thing I don't understand: If Lord Spencer had planned to kill Philip Havisham all along why did he cause such a fuss at the Criterion? He must have surely expected to be our main suspect."

"Good question, Sergeant. There are a few things which don't quite fit into the picture yet. If SW happens to be his fiancée then it would certainly explain why he had so eagerly searched for the letters – he was in danger of being discovered. For some reason he must have known or at least assumed that they existed. In the meantime, though, I think the evidence we have is enough to put him into jail."

! *Übung 68: Was ist gemeint? Finden Sie den passenden Begriff!*

ÜBUNG 68

1. something you put a letter into: _____

2. something you put money into: _____

3. a place for criminals: _____

4. to be born again: _____

5. another word for to be: _____

6. to look for: _____

"There is also one more thing I don't quite understand."

"And what might that be, Sergeant?"

"Why did Philip Havisham go to so much bother as to hide these letters?"

"That is also a very good question. You are a born detective."

Sergeant Thompson grinned from ear to ear.

"I'm sure Lord Spencer will be able to explain a thing or two. Let's get back to the police station and question him. He should still be in jail where we left him yesterday evening after we caught him gambling."

As soon as Detective Carlyle and Sergeant Thompson entered the police station, Chief Inspector Gatsby came thundering towards them. Detective Carlyle noticed his face was redder than its usual colour. He knew he was in for some trouble.

"Detective Carlyle, into my office now!" yelled Chief Inspector Gatsby pointing his finger in the direction of his office door.

"And as for you, Sergeant Thompson, you'll be lucky if you're not demoted to the rank of constable…for life!" he shouted, now pointing his finger at him.

The two policemen just looked at each other. Sergeant Thompson shrugged and went over to greet his colleagues. Detective Carlyle disappeared into Chief Inspector Gatsby's office.

Übung 69: Übersetzen Sie die Imperative!

1. Hinsetzen! _____

2. Geh doch weg! _____

3. Bleib da! _____

4. Mache es richtig! _____

5. Genug davon! _____

6. Tu es nicht! _____

7. Kommen Sie her! _____

8. Nicht laufen! _____

9. Hören Sie damit auf! _____

10. Nicht jetzt! _____

ÜBUNG 69

"Sit down!" Chief Inspector Gatsby said in a harsh tone. "So what's this I hear about you arresting Lord Fellowes and several other highly decorated citizens of London?"

"They were gambling, sir, what was I to do? It's against the law."

"What are you talking about? It was just a harmless game of cards amongst friends – that's what they told me!"

Detective Carlyle's eyebrow went up.

"A harmless game of cards in an old shed out in the docks, sir?"

Chief Inspector Gatsby thought the detective had a point.

"Maybe it's quiet out there. You know, away from wives and children," he said a little less harshly.

"Then why didn't they just go to the men's club?"

Chief Inspector Gatsby was not the most intelligent of persons. He felt he was beginning to lose ground and was starting to see that the explanation his club friends had given him was possibly not very plausible. He decided to slam his fist on his desk.

"Enough, I let them go this morning. I saw no reason to keep them here."

"You let them go?" Detective Carlyle could not believe his ears.

"Yes!" he replied as if it was the most normal thing in the world.

"How are you getting on with the Havisham case?" asked Chief Inspector Gatsby, trying to casually change the subject.

"Well, you've just let my main suspect go!"

"What – Lord Fellowes is your main suspect! Now listen to me…"

"No, no!" interrupted Detective Carlyle. "Lord Spencer is my main suspect."

"That isn't really much better!" growled Chief Inspector Gatsby. "I thought I told you to leave him alone."

"I found his wallet in the victim's house."

Chief Inspector Gatsby was lost for words.

Übung 70: Welche polizeilichen Begriffe werden gesucht?

1. the person who has been murdered:

_____

2. the person who is thought to have committed a crime:

_____

3. the general name for the process involved in solving a crime:

_____

4. the general word used for a person who is not guilty:

_____

5. the place where a criminal receives his sentence:

_____

"What did you say?"

"I said I found his wallet in Havisham's house. That proves he must have been there recently. It certainly wasn't there the last time I was there. We also have reason to believe his fiancée was having an affair with Mr Havisham."

Detective Carlyle's superior was now stunned.

"Oh…well…that seems to put things into a new light," he said a little more reserved.

"It's just a shame he's not around to question anymore. Would you mind if I just went back out to round up some men to go and arrest him?" asked Detective Carlyle in a casual, sardonic tone.

"No, I wouldn't mind!" answered Chief Inspector Gatsby unnerved. "Go and bring him in!"

"My pleasure, sir!" grinned Detective Carlyle.

Chief Inspector Gatsby sighed and motioned for him to leave.

Chapter 7: The Great Escape

Detective Carlyle, Sergeant Thompson and four constables arrived at Stephan's Hotel and went in. The landlord looked very astonished as the six policemen came towards him.

"Can…can…I help you?" he stuttered.

"Is Lord Spencer in his room?" asked Detective Carlyle.

"Yes!"

The landlord was going to ask something, but Detective Carlyle turned around and signalled his men to follow him up the stairs.

"He's in room 17," whispered Detective Carlyle. "I want you all to be as quiet as possible, I don't want him to escape."

! Übung 71: Lesen Sie weiter und setzen Sie die Wörter ein!
(gradually, sneaked, fault, hurt, carefully, approaching, him, hysterical, want)

The policemen (1.) _____ up the stairs. One of the constables stood on a rotted wooden step, it cracked. Everybody else looked at him. Sergeant Thompson shook his head. The young man just shrugged as if to say: "It's not my (2.) _____! How could I know?" The policemen moved on carefully until they reached Lord Spencer's room. Detective Carlyle signalled two of the constables to break down the door. He counted using his fingers: one, two, three…the policemen kicked the door open. Lord Spencer was sitting at his desk. He shot out of his chair with fright.

"What do you (3.) _____!" he cried and hastily opened one of the desk drawers and took something out. Detective Carlyle saw him doing this.

"Watch out! Seize him!" he shouted.

But it was too late – Lord Spencer was pointing a gun at them all. The policemen (4.) _____ moved back a little. Detective Carlyle stood closest to Lord Spencer. He held up his hands in a calming gesture.

"Put the gun down, Lord Spencer," he said firmly. "You do not want anybody to get (5.) _____, do you?"

Lord Spencer wiped sweat from his brow with his free hand.

"What do you want?" he asked again; this time in a more (6.) _____ tone. "Why can you not just leave me alone?"

"Now, calm down, Lord Spencer. We just have a few questions."

"Ha, a few questions, you say? Why did you bring half the London Police with you, if you just want to ask me a few questions?"

Lord Spencer was (7.) _____ moving backwards towards a window at the back of the room. One of the constables moved slightly towards his direction. Lord Spencer pointed the gun at (8.) _____. "Do not move or I will shoot you!" he shouted. Detective Carlyle signalled the policeman to stay where he was. Lord Spencer was (9.) _____ the open window.

"You are only making things worse," said Detective Carlyle.

"Making what worse, Detective? I did not do anything. You and your colleagues are driving me mad! Do you still believe I am the murderer?"

Detective Carlyle sighed and pointed at the gun.

"Well, Philip Havisham was shot dead with a gun similar to the one you are now pointing at us."

"I have had enough of your accusations, Detective," and with this Lord Spencer fired a shot into the air. The policemen ducked, plaster fell from the ceiling.

"I am not going back to jail!" he exclaimed and jumped out of the window.

! *Übung 72: Setzen Sie ein: do oder make?*

ÜBUNG 72

1. His behaviour is going to _____ things worse.

2. Sergeant Thompson had to _____ some research.

3. Lord Spencer said he did not _____ anything.

4. Detective Carlyle asked Sergeant Thompson to _____ him a cup of tea.

5. The baroness wanted Philip Havisham to _____ her happy.

6. The policemen had to _____ a lot of running.

"Is the man mad!" exclaimed Sergeant Thompson as the policemen rushed towards the window. They looked down. Lord Spencer had landed softly in the bushes that surrounded the hotel's premises. He freed himself from the bushes and ran. He accidentally dropped the gun and left it lying.

"Get him!" exclaimed Detective Carlyle.

The constables quickly left the hotel room. Sergeant Thompson wanted to join them, but Detective Carlyle held him back.

"Leave the chase to your men, Sergeant – I need you here."

Sergeant Thompson looked disappointed.

"But sir, that means I'm losing out on all the excitement," he sighed.

Detective Carlyle raised his eyebrow.

"I think we've had enough excitement for one day!" he said dryly.

"I saw Lord Spencer drop the gun. If it's a Remington Revolver then we have our murderer for sure. Let's go down and get it."

Übung 73: Wählen Sie die richtige Alternative!

1. The baroness laughed _____.
   a) ☐ hysterical   b) ☐ hysterically

2. Detective Carlyle was _____ prepared.
   a) ☐ well   b) ☐ good

3. Sergeant Thompson was _____ punched into the stomach.
   a) ☐ brutally   b) ☐ brutal

4. He said it in a _____ tone.
   a) ☐ dryly   b) ☐ dry

5. The policemen _____ ran down the stairs.
   a) ☐ fast   b) ☐ quickly

6. Lord Spencer was in _____ trouble.
   a) ☐ deeply   b) ☐ deep

7. The suspect _____ dropped the gun.
   a) ☐ accidental   b) ☐ accidentally

The two policemen walked out of the room. You could hear the constable's loud whistles in the distance. Some of the hotel guests had left their own rooms to see what all the commotion was about. They were standing around talking to each other. Some of them looked rather shocked. Just as Detective Carlyle and Sergeant Thompson were hurrying down the stairs, the landlord of Stephan's Hotel came running towards them.

Übung 74: Lesen Sie weiter und unterstreichen Sie im Text die gegenteiligen Begriffe der Wörter in Klammern!
(1. whispered, 2. brand new, 3. in front of, 4. doubtful, 5. far away from, 6. less, 7. everybody)

"What in heavens name is going on here? Who was shooting in my hotel?" he cried out.

"Oh, just the usual police affairs," answered Sergeant Thompson matter-of-factly.

"Who is going to pay for all the damage?" asked the landlord as he pointed at one of the rotted steps which now had broken under the weight of the running policemen.

"I'm sure Lord Spencer will pay for the damages," answered Detective Carlyle.

"Spencer?" laughed the landlord. "He never even has enough money to pay his rent!"

"Well, once he's behind bars I'm sure he will have enough time to save a pound or two."

"Jail – what do you mean by that? That man still owes me two weeks' rent," said the alarmed landlord.

"I'm more than certain you will read all about it in tomorrow's newspaper," answered Detective Carlyle.

The landlord sat down on a chair near the hotel exit. He shook his head and looked very worried.

"This is not good at all," he said more to himself. "After half of London has heard about this, no one is going to want to stay at my hotel."

Sergeant Thompson gave him an encouraging clap on the back and followed his superior out of the door. The policemen crossed the road. Detective Carlyle picked up the gun and examined it. He scratched his head thoughtfully.

"It's not a Remington Revolver," he said disappointedly.

"I think you're right, sir. It looks more like a Colt."

"And a Colt it is," sighed Detective Carlyle. "However, the fact the gun is a Colt still does not prove Lord Spencer's innocence in any way – but it sure would have made things easier if it had been a Remington."

Detective Carlyle gave Sergeant Thompson the gun.

"If you would kindly hold on to it, Sergeant?"

"Certainly, sir!"

The sergeant took the gun from Detective Carlyle and put it in his belt. Detective Carlyle gave him a disapproving look.

"Maybe you could be a little more discreet," said the detective.

Sergeant Thompson looked puzzled.

"Discreet? What do you mean, sir?"

Detective Carlyle nodded in the direction of the gun.

"We don't want the public to think that the London Police are now armed, do we?"

Sergeant Thompson looked down at the gun.

"Oh, yes, of course!" he answered feeling a little stupid.

He removed the gun from his belt and put it in the inside of his police uniform jacket.

Detective Carlyle nodded in a satisfied manner and smiled.

"That looks better – a policeman with a gun doesn't look like a friend and helper."

Sergeant Thompson smiled back.

"Now, Sergeant, let's get back to the police station and wait for your men to bring in Lord Spencer. He most certainly has a lot to answer for."

ÜBUNG 75

Übung 75: Setzen Sie die erste oder zweite Steigerungsform des Adjektivs ein!

1. Detective Carlyle wanted Sergeant Thompson to be (discreet) _____.

2. Detective Carlyle was (clever) _____ than Chief Inspector Gatsby.

3. Sergeant Thompson was (funny) _____ of all.

4. The case was (difficult) _____ than Detective Carlyle had thought.

5. Things were not getting (good) _____ for Lord Spencer.

6. Stewart Portman was (thin) _____ than Philip Havisham.

7. The lane was (narrow) _____ than the road.

8. Philip Havisham was the (nice) _____ person she had ever met.

Detective Carlyle was drinking a cup of tea in his office when suddenly the door opened. Constable Taylor entered:

"We've got him, sir."

"Very good work, Constable – would you kindly bring Lord Spencer into my office."

"Yes, sir!"

The constable turned around and was about to leave.

Übung 76: Setzen Sie das passende Pronomen ein!
(mine, his, your, them, him, me)

1. Detective Carlyle was drinking tea in _____ office.

2. "Shall I bring Lord Spencer, Baroness McKee and Simon Manlove into _____ office?"

3. "Oh no, not all of _____ at once!"

4. "I like Sergeant Thompson. He's a good colleague of _____."

5. "I tried to speak to him, but Lord Spencer did not want to talk to _____."

6. Constable Taylor said they had caught _____ soon after he had fled.

"Oh, Constable, due to all the commotion I nearly forgot: Did you find William Butcher to question him?"

"No, we didn't. He seems to have disappeared into thin air.

However, I talked to a colleague from Hyde Park Police Station, he told me they had locked up William Butcher the day Philip Havisham was murdered. He was behind bars all night because he had started a fight and had assaulted a policeman."

! *Übung 77: Lesen Sie weiter und fügen Sie das passende Wort ein!*
(handcuffed, take, again, best, dangerous, cause, returned)

"Well, if that's not the (1.) _____ alibi a man can have," Detective Carlyle laughed.

"You can surely say that (2.) _____, sir," chuckled Constable Taylor. "I'll bring Lord Spencer in then?"

"Yes, please do, Constable."

Constable Taylor (3.) _____ shortly afterwards with Lord Spencer. He pushed him carefully into the detective's office. Lord Spencer's hands were behind his back as he was (4.) _____. The policemen and the main suspect were followed by Sergeant Thompson. "You can (5.) _____ the handcuffs off," said Detective Carlyle. "But, sir, this man is (6.) _____!" protested Constable Taylor. "It's okay, Constable – I don't think Lord Spencer is going to (7.) _____ us any trouble…are you now?"

Detective Carlyle looked at Lord Spencer. He shook his head. Lord Spencer's face was dirty and his clothes were ripped – his attempt to escape had left some traces. Constable Taylor unlocked the handcuffs and sat Lord Spencer down on the chair at the opposite side of Detective Carlyle's desk. Constable Taylor stood there waiting for further instructions.

"You can leave now, Constable. Wait by the door in case Sergeant Thompson and I need any further help."

"Yes, sir! If you need any help with this rogue I'll be more than happy to lend a hand."

Constable Taylor gave Lord Spencer an angry look and left the office. Lord Spencer did not see this because his head was hanging down in resignation. He looked like a wild animal that had just been caught and given into its fate. Detective Carlyle felt very sorry for Lord Spencer. He looked over to Sergeant Thompson. He did not seem to share the same feeling. All the detective could read in his face was professional interest. Detective Carlyle opened a drawer, took out Lord Spencer's wallet and laid it on top of the desk.

Übung 78: Beantworten Sie die Fragen zum Text!

1. Why was the landlord of Stephan's Hotel so upset?

2. How did Lord Spencer escape?

3. How many times did Lord Spencer fire into the air?

4. Did Sergeant Thompson catch Lord Spencer?

5. What was Detective Carlyle doing before Lord Spencer was brought into his office?

6. Did Sergeant Thompson feel sorry for Lord Spencer?

_____

7. What did Detective Carlyle lay on his desk?

_____

"We found your wallet in Philip Havisham's house; could you possibly explain how it got there?"

Lord Spencer looked at Detective Carlyle for the first time. He shrugged helplessly.

"I have no idea," he answered. "It was stolen from me two days ago."

"Did you report it to the police?"

"No!" sighed Lord Spencer.

"Why not?"

"Well, to be honest, I had had more than enough of the police. As far as I was concerned I did not want to see the inside of a police station again for the rest of my life," he answered tiredly.

"That didn't keep you out for long, did it?" said Sergeant Thompson.

Lord Spencer ignored this and carried on:

"Secondly, there was not much money in it. Reporting it was not really worth the bother. As you can see for yourself, the wallet is not very new either." Lord Spencer paused for a moment and then said in a self-pitying tone: "Anyway, what use is a wallet to someone who has nothing to put in it."

"I'll just go and get the violin players, shall I?" said Sergeant Thompson sardonically.

Detective Carlyle silently signalled to the sergeant to keep statements like that to himself.

"So you say it was stolen?" Detective Carlyle proceeded with the questioning.

"I assumed so. I certainly do not understand how it got into Mr Havisham's house – I swear I was never there in my life!"

"Do you know a woman who has the initials SW?" asked Detective Carlyle, changing the subject.

"SW? No idea! Who is that supposed to be?"

"That is exactly what I am trying to find out. We found hidden love letters in Philip Havisham's house. I assume you were looking for them when you lost your wallet."

"I do not have the foggiest idea what you are talking about," said Lord Spencer in a more irritated tone.

"Coming back to life, are we?" asked Sergeant Thompson.

Detective Carlyle gave the sergeant a disapproving look. Sergeant Thompson made a gesture that he was sorry.

Übung 79: Setzen Sie das passende Adjektiv ein!
(difficult, sad, dishonest, helpful, low, narrow, immoral, unlucky, angry, lazy)

1. A person who kills is _____.

2. A person who cries is _____.

3. A person who lies is _____.

4. A person who shouts is _____.

5. A person who is out of luck is _____.

6. A lane that is not very wide is _____.

7. A task that is hard to solve is _____.

ÜBUNG 79

8. A person who always gets up late is _____.

9. A person who likes to help is _____.

10. A wall that is not very high is _____.

Lord Spencer was nervously playing with his hands. He looked up at Detective Carlyle:

"Would you please have the kindness to explain to me exactly what you are getting at?"

"We have reason to believe SW was or still is your fiancée...she had an affair with Philip Havisham…you eventually found this out and murdered him…"

Detective Carlyle could not finish his sentence as Lord Spencer was laughing out loud.

"Ha, ha, ha!" he did not seem to be able to stop. He gradually calmed down: "You should be writing crime stories, Detective Carlyle. This is getting better all the time: First you say I killed Mr Havisham because of his book and now you are saying I killed him out of jealousy. You certainly have a great imagination."

"Now, that's enough of your cheek!" protested Sergeant Thompson.

"It is okay, Sergeant. Let me deal with this," said Detective Carlyle calmly.

"So you are telling me you have never heard of a woman with the initials SW?"

"No! And she certainly was not my fiancée."

"You do know we can easily find out if you are lying to us."

"Go and find out!" spat Lord Spencer in disgust: "The sooner, the better!"

"If you are as innocent as you insist, why did you try and escape from the police? You did seem in great distress."

"Of course I was in great distress!" shouted Lord Spencer and rose up from his chair. It toppled over. Sergeant Thompson put his hand on his truncheon and moved closer.

"You just won't leave me alone. I tell you someone is trying to put the blame on me, can you not see that!" Lord Spencer cried.

The door opened. Constable Taylor looked in.

"Is everything all right?"

"Yes, thank you, Constable. Lord Spencer was just going to sit down again. I'm sure he doesn't want the handcuffs back on."

Lord Spencer sat back down and Constable Taylor closed the door again.

Übung 80: Welche Wörter gehören zusammen?

1. blame	☐ with
2. sit	☐ in
3. eat	☐ to
4. involved	☐ down
5. escort	☐ on
6. black	☐ up
7. stay	☐ out

ÜBUNG 80

"And what about my alibi?" asked Lord Spencer more calmly. "I do have an alibi, remember?"

"Yes, I remember very well. The problem with your alibi is that I do not trust the people connected to it. I believe they are trying to protect you. Minister Black lied to me many times, you know." Detective Carlyle paused. The office was absolutely silent. One could hear the voices and laughs of the policemen outside.

"I will ask you one more time: Who is SW?"

"I do not know, you must believe me!" pleaded Lord Spencer.

Detective Carlyle stood up and sighed:

"I'm afraid we're not really getting anywhere here, Sergeant. Would you kindly ask Constable Taylor to escort Lord Spencer back out."

Lord Spencer looked alarmed back and forth between Sergeant Thompson and Detective Carlyle.

"So that's it; you are locking me back up?" asked Lord Spencer.

"For the meantime anyway. There is just too much evidence against you, and your adventurous escape earlier today did not help to bolster your pleas of innocence."

Constable Taylor entered the office and led Lord Spencer back out. He did not protest or say another word.

"Poor chap", said Detective Carlyle regretfully, "what if he is innocent?"

"Looks like a liar to me, sir. I mean, he could have shot one of us today!" exclaimed the sergeant.

"He was aiming at the roof, Sergeant."

"How do you know for sure? Maybe he's just a bad marksman."

"Well, if he is a bad marksman, he certainly can't be the murderer of Philip Havisham – he was killed with one direct shot to the heart."

Sergeant Thompson scratched his head.

"You have a point there sir; maybe Lord Spencer was just lucky. You know, first time lucky sort of thing."

Detective Carlyle rolled his eyes.

"Where do we go from here?" asked Sergeant Thompson.

"We need to find out if Lord Spencer ever had or has a fiancée with the initials SW."

"Right, I'll get one of my men to make some inquiries – anything else?"

"Yes, ask Philip Havisham's friends, Simon Manlove, Stewart Portman and John Pirrip round to the police station – maybe they heard Philip Havisham talk about a woman with the initials SW."

Sergeant Thompson suddenly looked at Detective Carlyle as if he had been enlightened.

"I've got it!" he exclaimed.

"You've got what?" asked Detective Carlyle puzzled.

"I know what SW stands for!"

Detective Carlyle sat up in excitement.

"What?"

"Silly Woman!" laughed Sergeant Thompson.

Detective Carlyle smiled and made a half-heartedly disapproving gesture with his hands.

"Oh, get to work, Sergeant Thompson!" he laughed.

Übung 81: Enträtseln Sie die folgenden Definitionen!

ÜBUNG 81

1. the opposite of getting better: _____ (orsew)

2. another word for stupid: _____ (lilys)

3. a lot of action: _____ (nitocmomo)

4. during the investigation it is collected: _____ (viedecne)

5. to look into something: _____ (qiuerni)

6. not on purpose: _____ (cacdietnla)

7. owner of a hotel for example: _____ (droldnal)

Chapter 8: A Tragedy Unfolds

Simon Manlove, Stewart Portman and John Pirrip sat in Detective Carlyle's office waiting for him to arrive. The door opened and Sergeant Thompson looked in.

"Would anyone like a cup of tea?"

"No, thank you!" they all answered at once.

"Oh, well, fine with me. The detective will be with you in a minute."

Sergeant Thompson closed the door. The three friends looked a little out of place sitting in Detective Carlyle's office. Their exquisite clothes and upper-class behaviour stood out in contrast to his tatty and scarcely furnished office. The men's body language expressed a slight feeling of disgust. Stewart Portman especially showed great dislike of the place. He was sitting on the edge of his chair just touching the seat with his bottom. It looked as if somebody had forced him to sit on something very horrible.

ÜBUNG 82

Übung 82: Setzen Sie ein sinnvolles Synonym ein!
(maybe, disgusting, hot, certainly, discussion, shocked, replied)

"It's a ghastly place, is it not?" remarked Stewart Portman. "I have never been in a police station before."

"Well it is not quite Buckingham Palace," said Simon Manlove.

"Most (1. definitely) _____ not!" smirked Portman.

"Look at the furniture: The desk and chairs are populated with wood worm," he said screwing up his face.

"Yes, (2. revolting) _____! And look at the ceiling. It looks as if it might come down any second," said Simon Manlove.

"I wonder what Detective Carlyle wants?" asked John Pirrip, who was fed up with his friends (3. talk) _____ about the police station's interior.

"I have no idea – (4. perhaps) _____ he has found the murderer", (5. answered) _____ Simon Manlove.

"It is about time, if you ask me", stated Stewart Portman, "I wonder if it was that chap…ehm…Lord…what was his name again?"

"Lord Spencer," replied John Pirrip.

"Ah yes, Lord Spencer. I know his aunt. She must be absolutely (6. shaken) _____. Lord Spencer was always bad news, as far as I can remember anyway," said Stewart Portman in a matter-of-fact tone.

The office door opened and Detective Carlyle walked in. He had a (7. steaming) _____ cup of tea in his hand.

"Good afternoon, Gentlemen. I hope I did not keep you waiting too long."

Detective Carlyle sat down and smiled at the men. He looked over at Stewart Portman, who was still sitting on his chair in an awkward way.

"Comfortable?" asked Detective Carlyle.

"Most certainly, thank you", said Stewart Portman not very convincingly, "we were actually just talking about how cosy your little office is."

"Were you now," replied Detective Carlyle in a slightly suspicious tone.

Detective Carlyle opened one of his drawers and took out some biscuits.

"Does anybody want a biscuit?"

The three friends declined. The way they declined Detective Carlyle's offer one might have thought he had just offered them grilled ants. Detective Carlyle shrugged and took a bite of his biscuit and then took a sip of his tea.

Übung 83: *Lesen Sie weiter und tragen Sie die Vergangenheitsform der angegebenen Verben ein!*

"I guess, Gentlemen, you are wondering why you are here?"

"Yes, that is correct. We (1. think) _____ that maybe you had identified Philip Havisham's murderer," said John Pirrip.

"Well, we have a main suspect, we are just gathering evidence to make sure there is no doubt that he is guilty."

"Does the suspect have a name?" asked Simon Manlove.

"Yes, we have (2. arrest) _____ Lord Spencer."

"I knew it!" exclaimed Stewart Portman. "Don't like the man – never (3. do) _____!"

"Did you just call us into the police station to tell us that?" (4. ask) _____ John Pirrip.

"Well, as I was saying we still need to put some pieces together: I was wondering if Philip Havisham had ever (5. mention) _____ a woman with the initials SW?"

"SW?" asked Stewart Portman thoughtfully.

"Yes!"

"Our late friend had so many…how shall I say…lady friends…let me think…No, sorry, does not ring a bell."

"What about you, Mr Pirrip?"

John Pirrip (6. look) _____ a little pale.

"Is everything okay?" asked Detective Carlyle.

"Pardon?" he asked in a distant tone.

"I asked if everything is okay."

"Oh, yes, sorry, everything is fine. It is just a little stuffy in here. To answer your question: No, I am afraid not."

"It is strange, though," (7. remark) _____ Simon Manlove.

"What is strange?" asked Detective Carlyle.

"It is strange he never mentioned her. He always boasted about his lady acquaintances."

"That is interesting your saying that because we have reason to believe he was trying to keep this affair a secret."

"I wonder why?" said Stewart Portman. "That really was not like him."

The office door opened and Sergeant Thompson looked in.

"Do you have a minute, sir?"

Detective Carlyle nodded and said:

"If you would excuse me for a moment, Gentlemen."

Detective Carlyle went out of the office and closed the door behind him.

! *Übung 84: Setzen Sie, wenn notwendig, den richtigen unbestimmten Artikel ein!*

1. Do you know _____ woman with the initials SW?

2. Philip Havisham was shot half _____ hour ago.

3. Sergeant Thompson had _____ good news for Detective Carlyle.

4. Lord Spencer has run away from the police many _____ time.

5. Detective Carlyle is keeping _____ eye on Lord Spencer.

6. Stewart Portman has never been in _____ police station.

7. Simon Manlove is wearing _____ new pair of trousers.

8. Lord Spencer would pay _____ hundred thousand pounds to get out of jail.

9. Detective Carlyle needs _____ information.

10. Baroness McKee needs _____ advice.

"What is it, Sergeant?"

"My men just came back from their inquiry concerning the initials SW. It seems to be that Lord Spencer never had a fiancée with those initials. There was a Cassandra Anderson, however, nobody whose name consists of an S and a W."

"Oh dear!" exclaimed Detective Carlyle. "Maybe we have the wrong man after all."

"Or maybe the burglary and the letters are not connected to each other – a pure coincidence."

"But Lord Spencer's wallet was in the house and the house was broken into more than once."

Detective Carlyle scratched his head and sighed.

"This is a very tricky case. There is something missing…I just don't know what it is…something that is staring us right in the face, but we can't see it."

Detective Carlyle looked a little frustrated.

"I'll get back to my royal guests," he said sardonically. "I'll be with you in fifteen minutes."

1. pure	☐ life
2. real	☐ love
3. reality	☐ bread
4. plain	☐ bites
5. true	☐ mind
6. open	☐ coincidence

Sergeant Thompson nodded. Detective Carlyle opened his office door and entered. Just as he walked in John Pirrip nearly bumped into him.

"Oh, sorry!" he said.

"Are you leaving us, Mr Pirrip?" asked Detective Carlyle surprised.

"No, no! I just need some fresh air. I will be back soon."

John Pirrip walked out of the office. Detective Carlyle looked at Simon Manlove and Stewart Portman.

"Is everything all right with Mr Pirrip? He did seem somewhat upset."

"I do not know, Detective. He really has never been the same since his fiancée died last year and now Mr Havisham's death – maybe it is all getting a bit too much for him," replied Simon Manlove.

"How tragic!" said Detective Carlyle.

"Yes, very", stated Stewart Portman, "his fiancée actually drowned herself in the Thames."

"Oh dear, but why?"

"That is part of the tragedy – nobody really understands why."

1. John Pirrip sah sehr blass aus.

_____

2. Die drei Männer wollten keinen Tee.

_____

3. Simon Manlove hat noch nie von einer Frau mit den Initialen SW gehört.

_____

4. Er ist nicht mehr richtig derselbe, seitdem seine Verlobte gestorben ist.

_____

5. Stewart Portman fand das Büro von Detective Carlyle scheußlich.

_____

6. Nein, tut mir Leid, das sagt mir nichts.

_____

7. Detective Carlyle verließ das Büro und schloss die Tür hinter

sich.

_____

Detective Carlyle paused for a minute and stared thinking into his cup of tea. Simon Manlove and Stewart Portman exchanged looks. Suddenly Detective Carlyle looked up; his eyes were sparkling under his red, bushy eyebrows.

"Tell me, what was this woman's name?"

"Susan White," answered Simon Manlove.

"Susan White you say…SW…Susan White…that's it!" exclaimed Detective Carlyle.

The two men looked irritated.

"That is what?" asked Stewart Portman.

"The woman who wrote the letters to Philip Havisham was Susan White."

Übung 87: Welche Ausdrücke gehören zusammen?

1. cup of   ☐ chips
2. plate of   ☐ boxes
3. pile of   ☐ beer
4. bunch of   ☐ wine
5. glass of   ☐ tea
6. barrel of   ☐ flowers

"What letters?" asked Simon Manlove perplexed.

"We found love letters in Philip Havisham's house. They were signed SW," replied Detective Carlyle.

"You can not possibly believe Mr Havisham had something going on with one of his best friend's fiancées? I believe this to be a tragic coincidence!" exclaimed Stewart Portman.

"Yes, so do I!" said Simon Manlove. "Not even Philip could have done such a thing!"

"I would not be too sure there, Gentlemen," mumbled Detective Carlyle more to himself.

"Pardon, what did you say?"

Detective Carlyle shook his head.

"It was not important. Where exactly did Miss White drown herself?"

"She jumped from Vauxhall Bridge."

Detective Carlyle shot up.

"A most unlikely coincidence!" he exclaimed and hurried to the door. Simon Manlove and Stewart Portman got up. They looked very puzzled.

"But Detective Carlyle – I do not quite understand," said Simon Manlove.

"I will explain everything to you later."

!

Übung 88: Welcher Satz enthält die richtige Zeitform? Kreuzen Sie an!

1. Simon Manlove setzte sich hin.

   a) ☐ Simon Manlove had sat down.

   b) ☐ Simon Manlove sits down.

   c) ☐ Simon Manlove sat down.

2. Ich werde Ihnen alles später erklären.
   a) ☐ I will explain everything to you later.
   b) ☐ I will be explaining everything to you later.
   c) ☐ I was going to explain everything to you later.

3. Detective Carlyle starrte gerade nachdenklich aus dem Fenster.
   a) ☐ Detective Carlyle stares thoughtfully out of the window.
   b) ☐ Detective Carlyle was staring thoughtfully out of the window.
   c) ☐ Detective Carlyle stared thoughtfully out of the window.

4. Früher ging Philip Havisham ins Criterion.
   a) ☐ Philip Havisham was going to the Criterion early.
   b) ☐ Philip Havisham used to go to the Criterion.
   c) ☐ Philip Havisham went to the Criterion early.

5. Sergeant Thompson hat schon viele Lügen gehört.
   a) ☐ Sergeant Thompson has heard many lies.
   b) ☐ Sergeant Thompson heard many lies.
   c) ☐ Sergeant Thompson hears many lies.

Detective Carlyle hastily left his office. Outside he looked for Sergeant Thompson. Eventually he found him.

"Have you seen John Pirrip?" he asked urgently.

"The last time I saw him he was walking out onto the street; said he was going to get some fresh air."

Detective Carlyle ran out onto the street. He was closely followed by Sergeant Thompson. John Pirrip was gone.

"What's going on, sir?" he asked perplexed.

"I know who the murderer is!"

"Who?"

"John Pirrip!"

Sergeant Thompson looked very puzzled.

"John Pirrip?"

"Yes! Get your men together, Sergeant. We must find him – I'll explain everything to you later."

Sergeant Thompson hurried back into the police station.

ÜBUNG 89

*Übung 89: Füllen Sie die Lücken mit **do** oder **does**!*

1. _____ Philip Havisham really have many lady acquaintances?

2. _____ Detective Carlyle find John Pirrip?

3. _____ I know you?

4. _____ Detective Carlyle have a suspect?

5. How _____ you _____?

6. What _____ Philip Havisham say?

7. Why _____ Lady McKee hate Philip Havisham?

Detective Carlyle and Sergeant Thompson sat in the police coach. They were on their way to John Pirrip's house. The coach was travelling very fast. The two men were being jerked back and forth. Sergeant Thompson's police hat almost flew off. He caught it just in time.

ÜBUNG 90

Übung 90: Lesen Sie weiter und setzen Sie den gegenteiligen Begriff der Wörter in Klammern ein!

"So you believe SW and Susan White are the same person?"

(1. whispered) _____ Sergeant Thompson.

He had to speak very loud in order to make himself heard properly. The noise of the coach's wheels hitting the cobbled street and the rhythmic crack of the whip made a conversation very (2. easy) _____.

"Yes! John Pirrip must have found out about his fiancée's affair with Philip Havisham after her (3. life) _____. I assume if he had known about it (4. later) _____ he would have reacted sooner."

"He must have been shocked to hear of such (5. faithfulness) _____ – both his best friend and the woman he loved betraying him."

"You can say that again. Now we also understand why Philip Havisham hid the letters: He wanted to make sure his good friend John Pirrip would never find out."

"But how did he find it out eventually then?"

"I'm not quite sure. He possibly found something in his dead fiancée's belongings that made him suspicious; maybe even a letter. He obviously assumed there were more or he wouldn't have searched Havisham's house so often."

"Yes, he feared they would give him away, I believe."

"And he was right!"

"Remember the day we met him at Grosvenor Square?"

"Yes, he said he was on his way to the Royal Music Academy."

"I know, and how stupid of us not to realize that the academy is nowhere near Grosvenor Square."

"That's right. He probably had just been in Havisham's house to search for the letters again."

"And he left Lord Spencer's wallet there as well."

! *Übung 91: Lesen Sie weiter und setzen Sie das passende Wort ein!*
(reason, blame, hindsight, fooled, into, investigations, credit, exclaimed, assume, violin)

"He certainly had us (1.) _____, sir," said Sergeant Thompson angrily.

"He certainly did, Sergeant. For some (2.) _____ he must have found out that Lord Spencer was no longer our main suspect and tried to lead us back to him. He had planned all along to put the (3.) _____ on him."

"But how did he smuggle the gun and the cushion from Lord Spencer's hotel (4.) _____ the Criterion?"

"That is a good question: John Pirrip used his violin case – he had it with him all evening."

"His violin case…well, I'll be damned!" (5.) _____ Sergeant Thompson.

"I most certainly hope not," smiled Detective Carlyle.

"But, sir…how do you know that he did not hand in the (6.) _____ case?"

"I remember it lying by the fireplace beside the chair he was sitting on. He didn't have his coat or anything else with him; so I (7.) _____ he must have had it with him all evening."

"Come to think of it, that is very suspicious."

"Yes, in (8.) _____ it does. However, he had us very well distracted."

"He certainly did. We were concentrating the (9.) _____ far too much on Lord Spencer – the evidence was overwhelming though."

"Yes, I must give (10.) _____ to John Pirrip for that; he had everything very well planned."

"There is still just one thing I do not understand, sir."

"And what might that be, Sergeant?"

"How on earth did John Pirrip manage to leave the East Room of the Criterion unnoticed shortly after Philip Havisham with a violin case in his hand?"

"I thought about that too, Sergeant. Do you remember that Philip Havisham's favourite table was secluded from the rest of the room by a wooden screen?"

"Yes!"

Detective Carlyle took a piece of paper out of his pocket and unfolded it.

"The same night of the murder I got one of the constables to draw me a rough sketch of the Criterion…now look here…"

Detective Carlyle pointed at a room which was labelled "East Room". His finger moved along the paper.

"Do you see this small door? It's located right behind the table Philip Havisham and his friends dined at. You can't see it from the other tables because it is hidden behind the wooden screen."

Sergeant Thompson looked astounded.

1. dinner
2. jacket
3. waiter
4. paper
5. Victorian
6. dark
7. matches
8. pipe
9. case

☐ clothes
☐ smoke
☐ cigarette
☐ lane
☐ document
☐ London
☐ table
☐ pocket
☐ dine

"I see; the wooden screen prevented the other guests from seeing John Pirrip leave the room."

"Exactly! And nobody noticed he was gone."

"That was risky. A waiter could have come or theoretically someone could have seen him go through the door."

"That is absolutely correct, Sergeant. However, never forget: Crime is always connected to risk. There is no such thing as the perfect murder."

1. Susan White was pregnant. ☐
2. John Pirrip smuggled the gun into the Criterion in his violin case. ☐
3. One of the doors in the East Room was hidden by a wooden screen. ☐
4. John Pirrip gave his violin case to the waiter. ☐

5. Detective Carlyle knew that John Pirrip was not on his way to the Royal Music Academy. ☐

6. John Pirrip's murder plan was perfect and not risky at all. ☐

Detective Carlyle's eyes sparkled when he said this. He moved his finger onwards to the hall, drawn behind the door.

"Now, the side door leads to a quieter corridor of the restaurant – but nevertheless it also leads to the men's room and the Great Hall. John Pirrip was probably waiting for the right moment: He knew his friend liked to stay longer than the others; he also knew he would go to the men's room sooner or later."

"Well, sir, I must say you're a genius!" exclaimed Sergeant Thompson. Suddenly the coach went over a large bump. Sergeant Thompson fell on top of Detective Carlyle.

"Now, now, Sergeant; there is no need to get that exited!" Detective Carlyle laughed.

"Sorry, sir!" said Sergeant Thompson embarrassed and sat back on his side of the seat. Just then the coach came to a halt.

"That's us arrived!" called the coachman.

Übung 94: Lesen Sie weiter und fügen Sie die Übersetzung der angegebenen Wörter ein!

Detective Carlyle and Sergeant Thompson hurried out of the coach and ran towards the (1. Eingang) _____ of John Pirrip's house. They were followed by two other policemen, who had been travelling (2. neben) _____ the coachman. The door had not been properly closed.

ÜBUNG 94

"All right men, let's go in. But be (3. vorsichtig) _____,

John Pirrip could be armed."

The policemen carefully entered the house and searched the rooms.

All of a sudden one of the constables called his superiors.

"Over here!" he whispered.

The door to the bedroom was slightly open. John Pirrip was sitting

on a chair looking out the (4. Schlafzimmer) _____

window. He was holding a (5. Pistole) _____ to his

head – it was the Remington Revolver. Detective Carlyle took a

deep breath and entered the room.

"Mr Pirrip, at last we (6. gefunden) _____ you," he

said casually.

"What do you want?" asked John Pirrip turning around on his

(7. Stuhl) _____ nervously. "Leave me alone or I shall

shoot myself!"

Detective Carlyle signalled his men not to come into the room. He

carefully took a chair (8. in der Nähe von) _____

the door and sat down.

"Do not do anything rash, Mr Pirrip," he said calmly.

Sweat was running down John Pirrip's face and he was breathing heavily.

"But you know everything – I am going to be hanged sooner or later anyway!"

"Well, under the circumstances, you have a good chance escaping the death penalty."

"And spend the rest of my life in jail! I am better off dead!"

John Pirrip's finger pressed hard against the trigger.

"Goodbye, Detective!" said John Pirrip with a weary smile.

"No!" cried Detective Carlyle and jumped up from his chair. It was too late, John Pirrip had pulled the trigger, but nothing happened; the gun jammed. Detective Carlyle ran over to John Pirrip and pulled the gun from him. John Pirrip was going to attack him. Detective Carlyle's men came to his assistance. The two constables held John Pirrip back.

Übung 95: Ordnen Sie die Ausdrücke einander zu!

1. pull	☐ the coach
2. press	☐ the whip
3. push	☐ the menu
4. crack	☐ the button
5. throw	☐ the gun
6. fire	☐ the ball
7. read	☐ the trigger

"Let me go!" he shouted. "Let me go!"

Suddenly he stopped struggling and fell back onto the chair. He had no strength left in him.

Übung 96: Welche Wörter gehören zusammen?

1. drive   ☐ deeply
2. smile   ☐ highly
3. done   ☐ friendly
4. recommended   ☐ wearily
5. wink   ☐ well
6. sing   ☐ slowly

"Well, thank you very much for saving my life, Detective!" he said in an sardonic, weary tone. "Now I can either rot in jail or wait to be hanged."

"Let us wait and see what the court has to say to all of this."

"Tell me how you found out that Philip Havisham and your fiancée had had an affair."

John Pirrip took a deep breath.

"It was about a month ago. By chance I took one of her favourite books out of the library. I found a letter inside the book. It was addressed to Philip…"

John Pirrip's voice was shaky. He was trying hard not to cry.

"What did the letter say?" asked Detective Carlyle.

"Susan was…Susan was…writing to Philip threatening to kill herself, if he did not come back to her…she was scared he would leave her alone with the baby…"

Übung 97: Welche Wörter bezeichnen ähnliche Dinge?

1. dumb   ☐ preferred
2. try   ☐ positioned
3. shake   ☐ attempt

4. deep   ☐ novel
5. attack   ☐ opportunity
6. located   ☐ warn
7. favourite   ☐ bottomless
8. book   ☐ assault
9. threaten   ☐ tremble
10. chance   ☐ stupid

John Pirrip was fighting back his tears. The policemen standing around felt very sorry for this man. One of them shook his head. He could not believe what he was hearing.

"Did you have no idea this was going on?" asked Detective Carlyle. John Pirrip shook his head.

"Not in the least. I still cannot really believe it. I thought Susan loved me…after reading the letter the whole picture came together. Until then I just could not understand why she had killed herself…"

"When did you decide to kill Philip Havisham?"

"More or less straight away – he was an arrogant, self-centred, devious man and deserved nothing better. I wanted to revenge Susan…poor, dear Susan…and made a plan: I knew how much Lord Spencer hated Philip because of his book and I thought he would make a good suspect."

Übung 98: Vervollständigen Sie die Aussagen!

1. Sergeant Thompson hurried out of the coach and ran towards
   a) ☐ the entrance of John Pirrip's house.
   b) ☐ the back door of John Pirrip's house.
   c) ☐ the beautiful Baroness McKee.

2. Detective Carlyle signalled his men to
   a) ☐ come into the bedroom.
   b) ☐ keep out of the bedroom.
   c) ☐ overwhelm John Pirrip.

3. John Pirrip was fighting hard
   a) ☐ against his fears.
   b) ☐ against his anger.
   c) ☐ against his tears.

4. Detective Carlyle tried to stop John Pirrip
   a) ☐ from running away.
   b) ☐ from killing himself.
   c) ☐ from shooting him.

5. John Pirrip found one of his late fiancée's letters
   a) ☐ in Philip Havisham's house.
   b) ☐ whilst walking home one night.
   c) ☐ in one of her favourite books.

"So you shoved the note under his door telling him where to find Mr Havisham?"

"Yes!"

"And whilst you were at the hotel you also took one of the hotel's cushions!"

"Yes, it would have been a perfect plan…"

"…If it had not been for the letters," interrupted Detective Carlyle.

"Exactly, I knew some kind of correspondence must have existed, but I just could not find the letters. That shows you how afraid Philip was of anybody finding out about the affair; especially after Susan's death. My plan would have worked if you had not found the letters."

"Yes, that is the biggest weakness of committing a crime: Everybody believes they will never get caught."

Detective Carlyle looked at the two constables.

"Take Mr Pirrip back to the police station for further questioning. Sergeant Thompson and I will walk back. After the last few turbulent days we could do with some fresh air and a short break."

"Yes, sir!"

Übung 99: Ordnen Sie die Buchstaben zu einem sinnvollen Wort!

The constables (1. eld) _____ John Pirrip out of the bedroom and down the stairs. Detective Carlyle and Sergeant Thompson followed them. The constables seated John Pirrip in the (2. acohc) _____. One accompanied him inside and the other climbed up beside the coachman. The (3. piwh) _____ cracked and the coach shot off. John Pirrip looked very tired, but also somehow (4. lerieedv) _____. He waved wearily at the policemen standing at the side of the road. Detective Carlyle (5. ppitde) _____ his hat.

"Well, Sergeant, that's another (6. seca) _____ solved," he said watching the coach disappear into the (7. ecnastdi) _____.

"Yes, who would have thought it was him – he (8. yeanlr) _____ had us fooled into believing poor Lord Spencer had done it."

"It is the very perfection of a man, to find out his own imperfections," said Detective Carlyle thoughtfully.

"Who said that, sir?"

"St Augustine!"

"Oh, him again!" remarked Sergeant Thompson with a shrug.

He thought hard about something for a moment.

! *Übung 100: Was gab es bereits im Jahre 1879? Kreuzen Sie an!*

ÜBUNG 100

1. street lamps ☐
2. roller-skates ☐
3. radio ☐
4. telephone ☐
5. fish'n'chips shops ☐
6. bicycle ☐
7. car ☐
8. steam-boat ☐

"Come to think of it, St Augustine might have made quite a good detective himself," said the sergeant smiling at his superior.

"That could possibly be true, Sergeant," replied Detective Carlyle.

At the same time both policemen pointed to their noses – they laughed and began walking up the road.

THE END

Abschlusstest

Übung 1: Welche Synonyme gehören zusammen?

1. win   ☐ go in
2. enter   ☐ rush
3. hurry   ☐ argue
4. quarrel   ☐ smile
5. shake   ☐ attempt
6. try   ☐ succeed
7. grin   ☐ tremble

Übung 2: Fügen Sie die gesuchten Begriffe ein!

1. A person who serves in a restaurant is a _____.

2. _____ is the female equivalent of husband.

3. Detective Carlyle was _____ Edinburgh.

4. _____ John Pirrip left the East Room he killed

   Philip Havisham.

5. Something that happens by chance is a _____.

6. The opposite of after is _____.

7. They could not make _____ do it.

8. A place someone hides is also called a _____.

9. Lord Spencer was in _____ of trouble.

Übung 3: Was gehört zusammen? Bilden Sie sinnvolle Paare!

1. rowing	☐ stone
2. grave	☐ door
3. church	☐ flame
4. slam	☐ the case
5. burn	☐ guy
6. solve	☐ a fuss
7. make	☐ flowers
8. chap	☐ beer
9. barrel of	☐ boat
10. bunch of	☐ yard

Übung 4: Welcher Satz enthält die richtige Übersetzung?

1. Ich werde Ihnen alles später erklären.
   a) ☐ I will explain everything to you later.
   b) ☐ I was going to explain everything to you later.

2. Kommst du auch?
   a) ☐ Are you coming to?
   b) ☐ Are you coming, too?

3. Das gehört ihm.
   a) ☐ That belongs to him.
   b) ☐ That belongs to himself.

4. Philip Havisham war sehr gut angezogen.
   a) ☐ Philip Havisham was very good dressed.
   b) ☐ Philip Havisham was very well dressed.

5. Baronin McKee war nicht zu Hause.
   a) ☐ Baroness McKee was not in home.
   b) ☐ Baroness McKee was not at home.

Übung 5: Welches Wort ist das „schwarze Schaf"?

1. guy, man, chap, boy
2. poor, penniless, wealthy, broke
3. book, poster, notice, sign
4. lunch, dine, dinner, breakfast
5. tramp, beggar, well-to-do, poor
6. pale, white, ashen, blue
7. exit, leave, enter, go

Übung 6: Wandeln Sie die folgenden Ausdrücke in ihre weiblichen Pendants im Plural!

1. man   _____

2. husband   _____

3. baron   _____

4. policeman   _____

5. waiter   _____

6. host   _____

7. actor   _____

Übung 7: Welche Gegenteile gehören zusammen?

1. brand new
2. more
3. empty
4. cowardly
5. far away
6. safe
7. cover

☐ less
☐ bold
☐ near
☐ reveal
☐ dangerous
☐ crowded
☐ old

Übung 8: Unterstreichen Sie die richtige Alternative!

1. Chief Inspector Gatsby took a deep breath/gasp.
2. John Pirrip pulled/shoved the trigger.
3. Lord Spencer is nice/nicer than Philip Havisham.
4. Let us meet/meat at the hotel.
5. A piece/peace of paper lay on the ground.
6. Someone is trying to put the blame in/on him.
7. He rowed the boat onto/into the bridge.

Übung 9: Wie lauten die typisch viktorianischen Begriffe? Ordnen Sie die Buchstaben zu einem sinnvollen Wort!

1. moor-ntea   _____

2. pach   _____

3. terpat   _____

4. ris   _____

5. meadma   _____

6. ylads nma   _____

7. ginward-moro   _____

Übung 10: Setzen Sie, wenn notwendig, den passenden Artikel ein!

1. He warned him many _____ time.

2. Sergeant Thompson was _____ hour late.

3. John Pirrip was in _____ Great Hall.

4. Sergeant Thompson has got _____ news for his superior.

5. Lord Spencer needed _____ hundred pounds.

6. Philip Havisham did not like to get out of _____ bed.

7. Detective Carlyle ate _____ apple for breakfast.

Lösungen

Übung 1: 1. stairs 2. bright 3. room 4. pour 5. glasses 6. peace

Übung 2: rowing competition, Thames, river, water, boats, riverbank, landing stages, watermen

Übung 3: 1. crowded/empty 2. good/evil 3. mild/cold 4. bold/cowardly 5. long/ short 6. stop/move 7. win/lose

Übung 4: 1. coach 2. Victorian 3. bright 4. horse 5. it 6. house 7. because 8. father 9. peace 10. cost Lösung = aristocrat

Übung 5: 1. rowing boat 2. horse rider 3. coach driver 4. canoe paddle 5. ice skate 6. fishing net

Übung 6: 1. win/succeed 2. smile/grin 3. shout/cry 4. enter/go in 5. distant/far 6. good/excellent 7. close/near

Übung 7: 1. The restaurant is called Criterion. 2. He studies at the Royal Music Academy in London. 3. He plays the violin. 4. Well-to-do people dine at the Criterion. 5. He likes that it is cosy and private. 6. The waiter takes the coats to the cloak-room. 7. He sees an extremely attractive woman.

Übung 8: 1. waiter 2. musician 3. husband 4. boatman 5. royal 6. charm

Übung 9: 1. The restaurant only had three tables. 2. He heard their cheerful voices. 3. They drank a bottle of wine. 4. They say she used to be very beautiful in her time. 5. He read the menu. 6. Did you have any luck? 7. Mr Havisham lifted his glass.

Übung 10: 1. "Here's to you, Philip!" they shouted. 2. He flew into the evening sky. 3. Then he threw it onto the floor. 4. He was really happy they were leaving. 5. Afterwards his glass was full.

Übung 11: 1. His face was red with anger. 2. He calmly wiped his trousers. 3. He downed his wine in one. 4. This is no place for a quarrel. 5. The man tried to move towards him. 6. Nobody understood why. 7. He felt awkward.

Übung 12: 1. sad 2. grim 3. silly 4. tragic 5. short 6. awkward 7. dull

Übung 13: 1. accent 2. from 3. boss 4. tragedy 5. alongside 6. floor 7. open 8. heart

Übung 14: 1. smile 2. beggar 3. stand 4. leave 5. terrible 6. sad 7. silence 8. careless 9. happy 10. vulnerable

Übung 15: 1. to dine 2. to have lunch 3. to have breakfast 4. dinner 5. lunch 6. breakfast

Übung 16: 1. After 2. Before 3. After 4. before 5. Before 6. after

Übung 17: 1. popular/unpopular 2. important/unimportant 3. fictional/true 4. dangerous/safe 5. bitter/sweet 6. miserable/happy

Übung 18: 1. richtig 2. falsch 3. falsch 4. richtig 5. falsch 6. falsch 7. falsch

Übung 19: 1. Dr Brown wasn't sober. 2. He didn't lose his balance. 3. Detective Carlyle doesn't know who the murderer is. 4. The constables weren't listening. 5. The sergeant's men haven't found a clue.

Übung 20: 1. I can't 2. I'll 3. I don't 4. you're 5. we'll 6. it's 7. couldn't 8. I'm 9. he's 10. doesn't

Übung 21: 1. in front of 2. entered 3. hope 4. surprised 5. last night 6. money problems 7. eye 8. curious

Übung 22: 1. sea (see) 2. scrapps (scraps) 3. evning (evening) 4. new (knew) 5. peace (piece) 6. luke (look) 7. campain (campaign) 8. shoed (showed)

Übung 23: 1. on 2. over 3. in 4. under 5. at 6. near

Übung 24: 1. Lord Spencer received a message. 2. He (always) had visitors. 3. I can. 4. Yes, of course. 5. Yes, please. 6. I will come. 7. I (do) care.

Übung 25: 1. winged demon 2. gravestone 3. churchyard 4. house/home 5. locked door 6. overgrown garden 7. minister/cleric

Übung 26: 1. witnesses 2. doors 3. dresses 4. ladies 5. wives 6. halves 7. sheep 8. scarves 9. days 10. teeth

Übung 27: 1. too 2. to 3. to 4. too 5. too 6. too

Übung 28: 1. c 2. b 3. c 4. a 5. c 6. c

Übung 29: 1. hotel 2. duke 3. cathedral 4. typewriter 5. coincidence 6. sergeant 7. secret passage 8. lamp 9. minute 10. after

Übung 30: 1. Everything was neat. 2. He took a sip of tea. 3. Detective Carlyle closed the secret passage. 4. It suddenly bent down and plucked a flower. 5. The bright sun almost blinded him.

Übung 31: 1. stairs 2. grave 3. charge 4. good 5. arrive 6. collar 7. introduce 8. fast Lösung = sergeant

Übung 32: 1. b 2. b 3. a 4. b 5. b 6. b

Übung 33: 1. hurry/rush 2. honest/truthful 3. mock/scorn 4. assume/suppose 5. murderer/killer 6. conversation/talk 7. quarrel/argue 8. testify/bear witness 9. angry/annoyed 10. idea/suggestion

Übung 34: 1. next 2. called 3. as 4. his 5. about 6. all 7. at

Übung 35: 1. half past six 2. eight o'clock 3. quarter past four 4. ten past seven 5. twenty-five past ten 6. quarter to six 7. twenty-five to eight 8. ten to four 9. five past two 10. twenty past four

Übung 36: 1. hesitate/wait 2. slam/door 3. burn/flame 4. police/detective 5. murder/crime 6. ocean/calm 7. horse/coach

Übung 37: 1. impatiently 2. shouting 3. free 4. overwhelming 5. sooner 6. gun

Übung 38: 1. b 2. b 3. c 4. a 5. b 6. a 7. b

Übung 39: 1. richtig 2. falsch 3. falsch 4. richtig 5. richtig 6. falsch 7. falsch

Übung 40: 1. myself 2. yourself 3. himself 4. herself 5. itself 6. ourselves 7. yourselves 8. themselves

Übung 41: 1. solve the case 2. knock at the door 3. commit a murder 4. conduct an interview 5. eat a steak 6. make a fuss

Übung 42: 1. exclaimed 2. gasped 3. baffled 4. unbelievable

Übung 43: 1. Sir/Mr 2. chap/guy 3. Madame/Mrs 4. drawing-room/living-room 5. lady's man/womanizer 6. ante-room/foyer 7. patter/talk

Übung 44: 1. will 2. will 3. going to 4. going to 5. going to

Übung 45: 1. diary 2. hide-out 3. bedroom 4. constable 5. volunteer 6. murder weapon 7. a mess

Übung 46: 1. a lot of 2. a lot of 3. a lot of 4. much 5. much

Übung 47: 1. good 2. well 3. good 4. good 5. well. 6. good 7. well

Übung 48: 1. mislay 2. dread 3. wish 4. right 5. guilty 6. doubt 7. reveal 8. glad

Übung 49: 1. the 2. – 3. – 4. – 5. the 6. the

Übung 50: 1. c 2. a 3. b 4. b 5. c

Übung 51: 1. e 2. k 3. g 4. i 5. c 6. b 7. a 8. f 9. d 10. h

Übung 52: 1. shameful 2. shocking 3. disgraceful 4. despicable 5. appalling

Übung 53: 1. He had a relationship with a woman called Baroness McKee. 2. They had steaming cups of tea in front of them. 3. This place looks more like a fortress, if you ask me. 4. After he won her heart he left her. 5. Could Baroness McKee really murder a person? 6. Philip Havisham is a devious man. 7. He took a share of the diaries and sat at the corner of the bed. 8. Sergeant Thompson did not want to read the books.

Übung 54: 1. wish 2. investigating 3. observed 4. unnoticeable 5. statue 6. home 7. message 8. contact 9. luck

Übung 55: 1. stil (still) 2. wissdom (wisdom) 3. suden (sudden) 4. amuced (amused) 5. remot (remote) 6. dreem (dream) 7. meen (mean)

Übung 56: 1. a 2. b 3. c 4. b 5. a

Übung 57: 1. down 2. about 3. to 4. under 5. used 6. at 7. down 8. up 9. to 10. behind

Übung 58: 1. Who 2. Where 3. Whose 4. which 5. What 6. Who 7. Whose

Übung 59: 1. The baroness had a secretive aura. 2. They could not see into the room properly. 3. Sergeant Thompson put his hand into his inside pocket. 4. As soon as William Butcher leaves the café we will follow him. 5. The policemen carefully approached the boxes. 6. Detective Carlyle saw the curtain move.

Übung 60: 1. accusing 2. to be indiscreet 3. did you find out about 4. trust him 5. believe

Übung 61: 1. good-natured 2. leave 3. unspoken 4. penniless 5. sign 6. account 7. breakfast 8. age

Übung 62: 1. Baroness 2. Lady 3. Queen 4. Viscountess 5. Duchess 6. Princess

Übung 63: 1. who's 2. whose 3. that 4. who 5. which

Übung 64: 1. as soon as possible 2. chapter 3. senior 4. Great Britain 5. circa 6. before Christ

Übung 65: 1. minute 2. progress 3. pale 4. perplexed 5. understand 6. chuckle 7. jealousy 8. eager 9. victims 10. case Lösung = upper-class

Übung 66: 1. They were walking across Grosvenor Square. 2. He thought he could read his mind. 3. He found Lord Spencer's wallet. 4. He is late for his class at the Royal Music Academy. 5. He stuck it between the door's wooden frames. 6. He found him in the kitchen. 7. He was trying to pull up a wooden plank from the kitchen floor.

Übung 67: 1. say 2. him 3. yours 4. where 5. meet 6. by 7. about

Übung 68: 1. envelope 2. wallet 3. jail 4. reincarnation 5. exist 6. search

Übung 69: 1. Sit down! 2. Go away, will you! 3. Stay here! 4. Do it right! 5. Enough of this! 6. Don't do it! 7. Come here! 8. Don't run! 9. Stop it! 10. Not now!

Übung 70: 1. victim 2. suspect 3. investigation 4. innocent 5. court

Übung 71: 1. sneaked 2. fault 3. want 4. carefully 5. hurt 6. hysterical 7. gradually 8. him 9. approaching

Übung 72: 1. make 2. do 3. do 4. make 5. make 6. do

Übung 73: 1. b 2. a 3. a 4. b 5. b 6. b 7. b

Übung 74: 1. cried out 2. rotted 3. behind 4. certain 5. near 6. more 7. no one

Übung 75: 1. more discreet 2. cleverer 3. funniest 4. more difficult 5. better 6. thinner 7. narrower 8. nicest

Übung 76: 1. his 2. your 3. them 4. mine 5. me 6. him

Übung 77: 1. best 2. again 3. returned 4. handcuffed 5. take 6. dangerous 7. cause

Übung 78: 1. He was upset because some of his hotel interior had been destroyed. 2. He jumped out of the window. 3. He fired into the air once. 4. No, he didn't. 5. He was drinking a cup of tea. 6. No, he had more of a professional interest in him. 7. He lay Lord Spencer's wallet on the desk.

Übung 79: 1. immoral 2. sad 3. dishonest 4. angry 5. unlucky 6. narrow 7. difficult 8. lazy 9. helpful 10. low

Übung 80: 1. blame on 2. sit down 3. eat up 4. involved in 5. escort to 6. black out 7. stay with

Übung 81: 1. worse 2. silly 3. commotion 4. evidence 5. inquire 6. accidental 7. landlord

Übung 82: 1. certainly 2. disgusting 3. discussion 4. maybe 5. replied 6. shocked 7. hot

Übung 83: 1. thought 2. arrested 3. did 4. asked 5. mentioned 6. looked 7. remarked

Übung 84: 1. a 2. an 3. – 4. a 5. an 6. a 7. a 8. a 9. – 10. –

Übung 85: 1. pure coincidence 2. real life 3. reality bites 4. plain bread 5. true love 6. open mind

Übung 86: 1. John Pirrip looked very pale. 2. The three men did not want tea. 3. Simon Manlove has never heard of a woman with the initials SW. 4. He has never been the same since his fiancée died. 5. Stewart Portman thought Detective Carlyle's office was horrible. 6. No, sorry, that does not ring a bell. 7. Detective Carlyle went out of the office and closed the door behind him.

Übung 87: 1. cup of tea 2. plate of chips 3. pile of boxes 4. bunch of flowers 5. glass of wine 6. barrel of beer

Übung 88: 1. c 2. a 3. b 4. b 5. a

Übung 89: 1. Does 2. Does 3. Do 4. Does 5. do/do 6. does 7. does

Übung 90: 1. shouted 2. difficult 3. death 4. earlier 5. unfaithfulness
Übung 91: 1. fooled 2. reason 3. blame 4. into 5. exclaimed 6. violin 7. assume 8. hindsight 9. investigations 10. credit
Übung 92: 1. dinner/dine 2. jacket/pocket 3. waiter/table 4. paper/document 5. Victorian London 6. dark lane 7. matches/cigarette 8. pipe/smoke 9. case/clothes
Übung 93: 1. richtig 2. richtig 3. richtig 4. falsch 5. falsch 6. falsch
Übung 94: 1. entrance 2. beside 3. careful 4. bedroom 5. gun 6. found 7. chair 8. near
Übung 95: 1. pull the trigger 2. press the button 3. push the coach 4. crack the whip 5. throw the ball 6. fire the gun 7. read the menu
Übung 96: 1. drive slowly 2. smile wearily 3. done well 4. recommended highly 5. wink friendly 6. sing deeply
Übung 97: 1. dumb/stupid 2. try/attempt 3. shake/tremble 4. deep/bottomless 5. attack/assault 6. located/positioned 7. favourite/preferred 8. book/novel 9. threaten/warn 10. chance/opportunity
Übung 98: 1. a 2. b 3. c 4. b 5. c
Übung 99: 1. led 2. coach 3. whip 4. relieved 5. tipped 6. case 7. distance 8. nearly
Übung 100: 1. richtig 2. richtig 3. falsch 4. richtig 5. richtig 6. richtig 7. falsch 8. richtig

Lösungen Abschlusstest

Übung 1: 1. win/succeed 2. enter/go in 3. hurry/rush 4. quarrel/argue 5. shake/tremble 6. try/attempt 7. grin/smile
Übung 2: 1. waiter 2. Wife 3. from 4. After 5. coincidence 6. before 7. themselves 8. hide-out 9. a lot of
Übung 3: 1. rowing boat 2. gravestone 3. churchyard 4. slam/door 5. burn/flame 6. solve the case 7. make a fuss 8. chap/guy 9. barrel of beer 10. bunch of flowers
Übung 4: 1. a 2. b 3. a 4. b 5. b
Übung 5: 1. boy 2. wealthy 3. book 4. dine 5. well-to-do 6. blue 7. enter
Übung 6: 1. women 2. wives 3. baronesses 4. policewomen 5. waitresses 6. hostesses 7. actresses
Übung 7: 1. brand new/old 2. more/less 3. empty/crowded 4. cowardly/bold 5. far away/near 6. safe/dangerous 7. cover/reveal
Übung 8: 1. breath 2. pulled 3. nicer 4. meet 5. piece 6. on 7. into
Übung 9: 1. ante-room 2. chap 3. patter 4. sir 5. madame 6. lady's man 7. drawing-room
Übung 10: 1. a 2. an 3. the 4. – 5. a 6. – 7. an